THE
LANGUAGE
WARRIOR'S
MANIFESTO

THE
LANGUAGE
WARRIOR'S
MANIFESTO

How to Keep Our
Languages Alive
No Matter the Odds

ANTON TREUER

MINNESOTA
HISTORICAL
SOCIETY PRESS

mnhspress.org

The Minnesota Historical Society Press is a member of the Association of University Presses.

Manufactured in the United States of America

10 9 8 7 6 5 4 3

∞ The paper used in this publication meets the minimum requirements of the American National Standard for Information Sciences—Permanence for Printed Library Materials, ANSI Z39.48–1984.

International Standard Book Number
ISBN: 978-1-68134-154-5 (paper)
ISBN: 978-1-68134-155-2 (e-book)

Library of Congress Cataloging-in-Publication Data available upon request.

This and other Minnesota Historical Society Press books are available from popular e-book vendors.

For Giizhigookwe,
my daughter, Madeline Treuer,
who taught me love at its deepest
and inspiration in the highest.
Gizaagi'in, daanis!

CONTENTS

||||||||||||||||||||||||||||

THE
LANGUAGE
WARRIOR'S
MANIFESTO

FINDING FIRE
IIIIIIIIIIIIIIIIIIIIIIIIIIIIIIIIIIIIIIIIIIIIIII

I AM NOT A LIKELY CANDIDATE FOR TEACHING, OR EVEN HAVING much to say about, our language and ways. My father, Robert Treuer, was a white man who spoke nothing but German the first thirteen years of his life. My mother, Margaret Treuer, is Ojibwe and grew up in the heart of the Leech Lake Reservation, but like many in her generation, she was the child of parents who spent their formative years in residential boarding schools, where the language was forbidden. Her family experienced hard living, incredible poverty, and the beauties and struggles of reservation life during the Great Depression and World War II. For generations, nobody in my family and few in my community had received their Ojibwe language and culture as a birthright. I never attended a school that had a real tribal language program. Today I should not know my language, culture, or ceremonies.

But I do know my language, culture, and ceremonies. I speak Ojibwe fluently. I'm not as eloquent as some of our great surviving speakers today. But I officiate at our Medicine Dance, telling legends that are hours long entirely in Ojibwe. I routinely converse in Ojibwe with great speakers from all over Minnesota, Wisconsin, Michigan, Ontario, and Manitoba. I've written books in Ojibwe. I dream in my language.

And I am not alone. On the Lac Courte Oreilles Reservation in Wisconsin, a number of families, teachers, and other language activists have done something that hasn't been done there since World War II: they raised a child who speaks Ojibwe as a first language. And it's not just one child, it's over one hundred. They speak our tribal language, a language that most of their parents and grandparents do not speak.

My story and the story of communities like Lac Courte Oreilles are not isolated developments. They are part of an upswell, a resurgence, a revitalization of indigenous languages and cultures started by language warriors in many places. Their stories are incredible. They are inspiring. And they point the way.

I have a personal narrative to share with you. I share it not because I see any superlative significance in my accomplishments, but because I know my story and I believe it can impact yours. I also share it because in my connections to the journeys and wisdom of others who are deeply engaged in this work, I have found cause for hope and tools to do the work. Our languages can live.

Five hundred years ago, Europeans came to America and announced, "Those Indians ain't gonna last." They've kept saying it every year since. And for five hundred years in a row, the Europeans have been wrong. There is nothing as powerful as a living tribal language to prove that point. One of my mentors, the late, great Thomas Stillday of Ponemah, Minnesota, always had a poignant way to do it. I convinced some of the administrators at Bemidji State University, where I work, to bring him in to give the keynote speech at our annual American Indian Awards Banquet. He immediately broke all the rules for banquet speeches, which are supposed to be short, include a couple of good jokes, and focus on the students.

He spoke for over an hour and a half, and he did the whole thing in Ojibwe. When he was done, he said only one thing in English: "All you people who study Indians, study that!" And then he sat down. Although the eyes of many people at the event had thoroughly glazed over during his speech because they were monolingual English speakers, his message must never be forgotten. Our languages live. And although many of our own people do not speak our languages, through no fault of their own, the keys to accessing and understanding indigenous thought are our natural instruments of human speech—indigenous languages.

All humans have ancestors. But most immigrants, especially in a place like America, are disconnected from them. Most people know their parents and grandparents, and the names of their great-grandparents. But beyond that, they usually don't know their ancestors' names or even where they are buried. My relatives have been buried in the Bena Cemetery on the Leech Lake Reservation since before America was a country. That makes it hard to sell the family farm and move to California. But for white Americans, that's how it's done. If the job is in California, people move. They celebrate the freedom to have a malleable identity—to become Californian. When their kids move to different states, far from the parents, they try to keep it real with their grandkids through Facebook and FaceTime. Over time, the connections to place and across generations weaken.

Severing the connections to place and across generations is usually harder for Indigenous people. It was for me. My family tree is full of celebrated Ojibwe leaders like White Fisher and the very long-lived John Smith. I didn't have tools to analyze this when I was a kid, but as I got older it bothered me more and more that I was sent to school for thirteen years, ostensibly to learn everything I needed to know to be successful in the world, and none of it had anything to do with *me*. The message was clear: "You and yours are not important, not significant, and of no value." This simply continues the age-old assaults on tribal language, culture, and identity. It was an assault on me. I felt terribly isolated and alienated when I was young.

I leveraged that into unflappable motivation as I grew.

My maternal grandmother, Luella Seelye, was a product of residential boarding schools. Every year from 1879 through World War II, the US government brought twenty thousand Native kids to these schools, deliberately forbidding them to speak tribal languages, imposing harsh physical discipline, and providing little nurture. These schools dominated Native American education through the 1950s. There are still some in operation today at places like Flandreau, South Dakota, and Wahpeton, North Dakota, although they no longer beat people for speaking tribal languages.

The Canadian government did the same thing—with many schools still operating into the 1990s. Many children learned to be ashamed of their language and their culture. Luella survived, came home, and raised a family. But she did that in English, rather than Ojibwe. The fluent Ojibwe spoken by her mother, Isabelle Matthews, was not passed on to her kids or to me.

My father, Robert, was an Austrian Jewish immigrant and Holocaust survivor. He was chased around the streets of Vienna by Hitler Youth and barely escaped with his life. Both of his parents and two of his cousins also survived, but more than three hundred other immediate family members were killed in streets and the camps. His is an incredible story, but that's another book. He made his way to Minnesota, met my mom, and here I am.

My mother grew up in a close-knit and supportive commu-nity that was often defined by endemic poverty. She got ice cream once a year. Everyone had to harvest wild rice, not because it was a cool, cultural pastime but because it was a necessary means of survival. When my parents were getting together, my dad was hitting the restart button, which he did several times in his life: after the Holocaust, after enlisting in the US Army at age seventeen, and after his first marriage failed. And my mother was trying to find a pathway out of poverty.

They did fine by me. I never had food insecurity or struggles that compared to theirs. My folks were on a transformative life journey of their own. Our cabin in northern Minnesota had a kerosene lantern, no running water, a hand pump, and an outhouse. We washed up in the creek in the summer and in enamel wash basins in the winter. But at the same time, my mother pursued a law degree in Washington, DC, which is where I was born in 1969. For several years, we spent summers in that rustic cabin, and then school years in Washington. I went back and forth between being an Indian and being *the* Indian. It was sometimes confusing and painful, but often beautiful too.

My mother eventually became the first female Native attorney in the state of Minnesota. In 1977, we moved home to Ojibwe country for good as she opened a private law practice and then became a tribal judge. This revealed to me the power of an education. The world does not distribute "barriers" and "boosts" equitably. Some people have it harder than others, and there is a race and gender predictability to the distribution of those barriers. An education is a powerful lever that improves—but doesn't guarantee—the chances that someone can overcome adversity and make it in spite of the barriers. The myth of the American dream really is a myth. As George Carlin said, "They call it the American Dream because you have to be asleep to believe it."[1] But in spite of all that, by the time I hit middle school, my mother had built a nice house, and the economic profile of our family started to change dramatically.

My father, even before he met my mom, had acquired a large piece of acreage just off the reservation, for very little money. It had been taken in a tax forfeiture and was sold with sealed bids. His was the only offer, and it wasn't even sufficient to cover the delinquent taxes. The land had been virgin pine forest generations before, but it had been clear-cut and turned into farm fields. He started planting trees. Today it is hundreds of acres of tall pine trees. He—one man, with a child labor force—completely transformed the landscape and ecosystem. When I look out my window at the forest he planted and wonder how we can revitalize the Ojibwe language after all the damage that has been done to it and us, I just remember: We don't have to move that mountain in one day. We just have to keep planting the seeds. We really can change everything.

As I grew up, I had many blessings, including access to parts of my indigenous culture that many did not. My dad, having been uprooted from his homeland and transplanted into a Native space, was eager to adopt what he could of that lifestyle. And even when my mom left the rez, the rez never left her. So we grew up hunting, fishing, picking rice, and making maple syrup and sugar. We never lived off the grid, but we knew how to get food. My mom regularly attended tribal ceremonies, and she brought me with. I heard our language and music, and listened to our elders giving long speeches or gossiping in the summer shade.

My mom worked. My dad worked, and then stayed home to write books and raise kids. I went to school. In spite of my experiences with food sovereignty and cultural practices, I never had enough exposure to our language to learn more than a few words. My peers in Washington, DC, and Bemidji were mainly white, and everyone in my social and educational circles spoke English only. I always felt like I was on the outside looking in.

I was a great novelty at Murch Elementary School in Washington. Everyone in my class was either white or black, but I was brown—and a boy with long hair. It was 1975. One day my first-grade teacher decided to dress me up like a girl in front of class, with barrettes, makeup, and all. Everyone had a good laugh. I come from a long line of ferocious warriors, so there was no way I was going to cry about that. But I did come home and tell my mom, "I want a haircut." And I got one. I didn't tell her why until I was an adult.

My second-grade teacher was black. She was the only teacher of color I had from kindergarten through my master's studies, up until I started to work on my PhD. And she treated me like a normal kid. I was so relieved, that—even though I'm right-handed—I tried to write left-handed, because she was a lefty. But then came third grade and white teachers every single year thereafter. I froze. Rather than suffer another humiliation at the hands of my teachers, I decided to put on my best stoic Indian face. For the first several weeks of third grade I refused to speak. They kept sending me to the principal's office, to speech pathology, and to special education. And I never spoke a word to any of them. That is, until they threatened to kick me out of school and asked, "Do your parents speak languages at home, other than English?" Fearing my mother's potential response to that consequence, I blurted out, "Dad speaks German. Mom speaks Ojibwe." They both spoke English perfectly, but the school had no way to know that. So they called my folks in for a conference and began to ask questions, speaking at high volume with deliberate slowness. My mother said something snarky and annoying to the administrators and then snapped around and gave me the Indian-mother-Godzilla-laser-vision-death-stare, and I started to speak. My experience that one day in first grade had deeply shaped my classroom behavior and worldview for three years. Not everyone has a day like I did in first grade, but a lot of our people have other painfully transformative days.

I struggled through the next years at school, being spoon-fed out of a bucket of whiteness every day. I found ambition, pursued a formal education after high school and beyond, but I knew I was just buying time and building credentials. I was subversive, contrarian, driven, and ready to do something big and bold. I wanted to turn the whole educational system of torture on its head. I just needed to find the way.

THE IMPORTANCE OF LANGUAGE

||||||||||||||||||||||||||||||||||||||||||||||||||||||||||||||||||||||||||||||||||||||||||||||

PEOPLE CHANGE OVER TIME. NO HUMAN CULTURE OR LANGUAGE is static, or frozen in time. Even for those who have tried to slow the pace of change, change is inevitable. The Amish pay taxes to the United States of America and are economically integrated into the world economy; people leave their communities, and sometimes new people join. I have never met an elder from any culture who did not shake his or her head and say, "Kids these days." Those elders complain about cell phones and social media, the way people dress now, and changing mores. There is a tension about cultural change. Change in and of itself can be good—like innovations in health care. And it can be bad—like the loss of a language, or a major degradation of the environment. And it can also be something in between. Human societies are like water rushing down a mountain—we follow the gorges and paths of least resistance. For many there is little alternative but to follow the choices of their families and communities. For others, even where religious preferences and values might not be dictated by one's parents, choices often stem from them as people follow those well-trodden paths. The water is always rushing downward. Once in a great while, someone stands in the torrent and diverts the flow to a new channel. Humans are always changing. But it is possible to shape the change.

Revitalizing a language that is not one of the world's one hundred most commonly spoken and taught requires special effort. The deck is stacked against us. Such a phenomenal undertaking never happens by itself simply because it is deserved or right, or because people wish it would happen. It takes real, intentional effort. And such intentional effort also requires leadership. Leadership like that is not found, it is made. We have to provide the initiative ourselves—nobody can or will do it for us. We cannot wish our languages back to health. We cannot teach them if we don't first learn them. We can't lead in their revitalization from the sidelines.

Uncle Sam is never going to come walking out of the bush or over the Plains and hand you your language on a silver platter, saying, "Sorry about the last five hundred years." The world is not a fair place. Fairness is not given, it is made. So we have to engineer it ourselves.

As we strive to make our own luck, to generate agency, and to manifest sovereignty, we have to sift through numerous competing priorities—health, economics, substance abuse, suicide, politics, and oil pipeline fights. All too often, tribal language and culture are seen as luxuries, or as important concerns that are never quite important enough to be funded, supported, and prioritized consistently in our individual lives or collective endeavors. As we seek to shape the change, we first have to see and explain to the world why language revitalization is important. Language warriors see the importance of their language, center their lives around it, and lead the effort to bring it back.

There is no way to convince everyone to support the revitalization of our languages, so laying out reasons for our efforts does not mean we wait for them all to join the movement. We act and advocate at the same time. The acting is required to combat inertia. We don't have time to waste. And the advocating is to make sure the effort is not done in isolation or without support.

* * *

Many humans from many cultures feel lost and disconnected. The pace of change is accelerating through technological innovation and interconnectedness. Connections to motherland, mother tongue, and mother culture are deluged by a sea of information, pressure on everyone's time, and huge institutions (political and religious) that script our opportunities for meaning and action. For many of us in indigenous spaces, this is true as well, but because we are in distinct communities surrounded by this sea of rapidly changing culture, the pace of change for us is in many ways even more pronounced.

Human identity is shaped by many things. In a postcolonial world, skin color—"race"—still has major effects on how we live our lives. We get "othered" first by how we look. But race is also about culture. A black Haitian who speaks French-Creole, a black Dominican who speaks Spanish, and an African American who speaks English might appear similar at first glance, but their cultural and linguistic distinctions are profound. The same is true of a Luxembourger, a Pole, and a Swede.

This works the same way in indigenous space. In the United States alone, there are 573 federally recognized tribes and many others that are not recognized. Their languages are often radically different and in varying degrees of health, ranging from completely extinct to having more than 150,000 remaining speakers. Racial identity is also partially about consciousness, or how we see ourselves. Many Native people look white or look black but have a strong indigenous identity. And lots of brown folks don't see indigenous blood when they look in the mirror because their cultural associations (being Latinx, for example) trump their biological ones, and their consciousness is not always indigenous. In the Latinx communities of the world, this is changing fast. But for Indigenous people, navigating race is complicated—in color, in culture, and in consciousness. And nothing grounds a person or a community more powerfully in indigeneity than carrying the tribal language. It is formative to racial consciousness.

Our connection to place is also a powerful and formative part of our identity. For me, living in my community and having my relatives buried in the same place longer than the United States has been a country is a big piece of who I am. But half the tribal population lives off-reservation. The government tried to get us out of our communities through the Indian Relocation Act of 1956, when they provided one-way transportation to cities to entice reservation Indians to become urban. We have moved around voluntarily, too, searching for jobs and marrying people from other tribes and races. We are complicated. And we become who we hang out with, for better and for worse.

Indigenous languages can thrive in urban areas too, from Navajo towns to Hilo, Hawaii. But the language is the conduit that can bridge the disconnections most of us experience in this complex world. We can hang out with our folk, create community through language, and be better grounded in our Native roots with the Native people who have similar struggles, dreams, and triumphs.

Our identity crisis also extends into other realms, like culture and customs. Here too, we face a deep challenge to our indigenous identities. Most of us are familiar with cars, but few of us are at ease in a canoe, on a horse, or setting a trap for beaver. While we get to learn new customs, to be modern, we also become more westernized, as the modern associations we have were largely created by non-Native people. But when we deeply engage in our language communities, we can decolonize that process. We can learn how our ancestors saw the world, greeted one another, ate, and made decisions. Language lets us connect to, rather than disconnect from, our cultural patrimony and customs.

Everything about being Native has been under assault for generations, even our food. For my tribe, the Ojibwe, our staples before contact were wild rice, blueberries, and wild game and fish (boiled, not fried). Confined to small remnants of our traditional homeland and given rations of lard and flour, Ojibwe and other Indigenous peoples figured out how to make fry bread—high in fat and high in its glycemic load. They survived, at least some of them. And today Indigenous Americans have the highest diabetes rate of any ethnic group on the planet. We have to change that by re-indigenizing our diets. Language and culture go hand in hand, so a meaningful language revitalization effort will necessarily force a reimagining and reconstructing of everything, including our food. It can help us live longer.

Native Americans have distinct political entities with more than a vestigial remnant of our precontact sovereignty. But our current systems of governance and citizenship are built by non-Natives and modeled after their systems. While this is starting to change, the infusion of language into such an effort is critical to our identity and self-perception. No matter what your enrollment status is, if you know your language, you know who you are.

* * *

In Ojibwe, we have a word—*inwe*—which we use for language. *Inwe* means "he or she speaks a certain language," and the roots of the word say it all: *we* means "to make a sound" and *in* means "in a certain way." So *inwe* means "to make a characteristic sound." In Ojibwe, all sentient life can inwe. A dog will inwe with a bark. A cat will inwe with a meow. So how then does an Ojibwe person inwe? It's not in English; it's in Ojibwe. The language is our characteristic sound. And if we lose that sound, we risk losing a central piece of what makes us Ojibwe and keeps us identifiable to our ancestors.

One-third of the white folks in my home state of Minnesota are of German heritage, and most of their families have been here for five generations now. They do not speak German. Most have never been to Germany. If they do go, they have a nice visit and then return to Minnesota, where they feel most comfortable and at home. There is a difference between having German blood and being a Deutschländer. So, too, is there a difference between having Native blood and being what our ancestors were. I strongly advocate for changing over time. An Anglo-Saxon English citizen descended from someone who saw the premiere of an original Shakespeare play doesn't have to worship at Stonehenge to be authentically English today. And that should be the same for us. But how much can a people change and still be the same people?

Languages themselves change over time—and more rapidly than most people realize. I can barely read Geoffrey Chaucer's works because English has changed so much over the past six hundred years. But in spite of these changes, the English language retains a continuity of thought, worldview, and identity. It grounds and informs an English person's sense of self. The same is true for other people and other languages. There are surely variations in the worldviews of different

English-speaking peoples around the world, but there are continuities as well that transcend bloodlines. A language provides a unique worldview and identity.

There is a vibrant discussion in the growing field of Native American literature about what makes something *Native American* literature. On the one hand, the writers are Native, and they often explore their identity in their work, even works of fiction. They use their personal experiences to inform their work, but they also talk about things like blood memory, an inherited cultural authenticity, and distinction. These are exciting and powerful works. But on the other hand, almost all of the writing is being done in the English language, using an English literary form: the novel. It is directed at non-Native audiences who often appreciate the novelty of the Native characters and storylines but also their relatability to distinctively white experiences. Is that Native American literature, or is it English literature produced by Native people? And don't forget that we do have our own literature—oral histories, legends, and songs. Those things are produced and transmitted in indigenous languages and indigenous contexts for indigenous audiences. I support all of these forms of literature and their authors. I think it's really dangerous to try to out-Indian one another. And it's painful for those who feel criticized or marginalized by the debates. But indigenous languages carry a higher level of authenticity for accessing, exploring, and sharing things in and about Native worldviews and experiences in the past, present, and future.

*   *   *

Some people think Indians are history and nothing more. We are "the last of the [blank]," with the word *blank* being the name of whatever tribe is under discussion. But using an indigenous language says we are ancient and modern, thousands of years of documented human history still in the making. That message is critical to combatting the marginalization and invisibility that our people often face in the eyes of the rest of the world. But it is even more critical to fighting off the marginalization and invisibility we so often internalize and inflict upon ourselves and one another.

Hodding Carter once quoted a woman he called "wise," who said, "There are but two lasting bequests we can hope to give our children. The first of these is roots; the other—wings." In the white world, the emphasis is usually placed on wings— individual accomplishment, competitiveness, and materialism. People often lead rootless lives, pursuing money and status. But roots are critical to all people, especially in indigenous communities. They define what it means to be indigenous, a native of a particular place since time immemorial. The language is a powerful glue that cements these connections.

Languages embody unique worldviews. This is obvious to me every time I operate in Ojibwe. In Ojibwe, the roots of words are usually known to everyday speakers of the language. Fluent speakers often remark that things are funnier in Ojibwe because each word has its association (action, person, place, thing, condition) and its deeper meaning. And they will say that, when telling a story, it's like someone is painting a picture. The language is loaded with thick description.

In Ojibwe, for example, we have a belief that the body is a cup—temporary housing for the soul. We aren't humans looking for a spiritual experience; we are spirits having a temporary human experience, and this understanding is embedded in the language. *Niiyaw*, meaning "my body," is literally "my vessel." When someone gives someone else an Indian name, the name usually comes from a dream or vision obtained while fasting. It comes out of the name-giver's vessel and is put into the name-receiver. So *niiyaw* means "my body," and *niiyawe'enh* means "my namesake." Both have the same root, *yaw*, in reference to the vessel. The namesakes have two vessels with a shared spiritual connection and hold the same dream or vision.

In Ojibwe, the word for elder, *gichi-aya'aa*, literally means "great being." The word for elder woman, *mindimooye*, means "one who holds us together" and describes the role of the family matriarch. You don't have to say things like "Respect your elders" when you're operating in Ojibwe. Every word used to talk about elders is loaded with respect. We often describe life cycles in stages of four: four directions, four seasons, and four stages in life—babies, young people, adults, and elders. The goal is not to stay twenty forever, or to fight wrinkles and gray hair with Botox injections, face-lifts, and hair dye. The goal, as expressed in Ojibwe ceremonies, is to see all stages—to live a long life, to be so old that you can't even crush a raspberry between your gums anymore. Elders are highly venerated. They eat before anyone else. Respect for elders just doesn't come across the same way in the English-speaking world.

There are many words in Ojibwe with the morpheme, or root, *de*: *ode'* (heart), *ode'imin* (strawberry), *oodena* (village), *dewe'igan* (drum), and *doodem* (clan). *De* means "heart" or "center." The heart is the center of the human body. A strawberry is a heart-shaped fruit. The village is the center of the people. The drum is the heartbeat of the people. Clan is the heart of someone's spiritual identity.

It is always fascinating to see how lexical expansion works in different languages. Just a couple of decades ago, an English speaker would have been confused or even startled by words like *motherboard* and *firewall*. The English language had to grow to describe new things. Indigenous languages have to do the same thing. In Ojibwe, lexical expansion is usually not accomplished with loan words or cognates from other languages but by creating new words with Ojibwe morphemes. So television is *mazinaatesijigan*, a "box that reflects an image through light." Even pants were new to the Ojibwe at one point, so people called them *giboodiyegwaazonag*, or "leggings that sew up the hind end." They must have seemed highly impractical to Ojibwe folks in a cold climate, when leggings and a breechclout (a skirt) gave you quick and easy access so you didn't have to freeze for too long when taking care of business.

Important cultural concepts often get lost in translation. In Ojibwe we often say "giga-waabamin miinawaa" when parting company. It means "I shall see you again." Simple though that is, it speaks to an important spiritual belief—that our souls are eternal even though our bodies are not. "Giga-waabamin miinawaa" says "I shall see you again" in this world or the next, and affirms the ever-living soul of the person being spoken to. It's different from saying "goodbye."

* * *

Our indigenous languages are a cornerstone of tribal sovereignty. If we are assimilated into the ruling class, by what right can we claim independent sovereignty within the territorial borders of the United States? Of course, we signed more than four hundred treaties with the US government, and those treaties are enshrined in the US Constitution as "the supreme law of the land." The federal government has a federal trust responsibility, articulated in those treaties, to safeguard our sovereignty and provide for the education and health of Native Americans. But the US government has always lied to Native Americans and often to everyone else. Consider that every time there is a new election, everything changes. One president and the congress he worked with promised free trade via the North American Free Trade Agreement (NAFTA), while the next said that agreement and promise meant nothing. The same is true with countless agreements in foreign policy, trade, taxes, entitlements, and other domestic affairs. This nation does not often keep its word.

In Ojibwe, our word for truth is *debwe*—literally meaning "to speak from the heart" or "heart sound." If someone says they will take care of someone else, that's a promise for life and across generations. But in white American culture, truth is not a heart sound, it's a fine-print version of legalese. The rental car company sells you insurance to cover damages but doesn't tell you until after you crash the car that the insurance you just bought doesn't kick in until after they have exhausted benefits from your primary auto-owner policy back home. Those details are buried in the legalese.

We use 250-year-old agreements to motivate current American presidents and members of Congress to honor our sovereignty, as well we should. But for a nation that has a history of ignoring and dishonoring its agreements, this is a vulnerable position. We are legally and morally right to fight for our sovereignty, but politically this is a heartbreakingly weak, slow, and unreliable form of leverage. But when we carry on our ancient customs and speak to our distinct nationhood in tribal languages, the message is poignant and powerful. It has genuine traction in politics and among our fellow non-Native citizens who vote the powerbrokers into office. We have a hard enough time convincing our own people that tribal sovereignty is important. Without our languages and cultures, convincing everyone else is a big lift.

The United Nations has been a recent point of contact for

tribes seeking international recognition, and the UN Declaration on the Rights of Indigenous Peoples is a powerful document even though it lacks enforcement in most places. But even the UN defines sovereignty as resting in a defined political entity with a sovereign land base, a living identifiable culture, and a living language (or languages). Here too, the language is leverage and we need it.

* * *

Countless studies back up the importance of both language learning and bilingualism. Bilingualism in particular predictably enhances academic achievement and cognitive function. Kids develop faster in both languages if they are bilingual. Too often, we ignore one of the most powerful tools in our arsenals for educational advancement.

The educational systems of Canada, the United States, and many other countries just do not work for their indigenous populations. In America, half of the Native kids do not meet the minimum standards in academic English and mathematics. Schools test those subjects every year and sculpt the entire curriculum around them. Half of the Native kids in America do not even finish high school. *Half.* The system is not working. In fact, only 60 percent of the students of color in America graduate from high school. And students of color now comprise the majority of the K–12 students in the United States. We know that the average income of a high-school dropout is $20,000 per year, while someone with a terminal degree—the highest degree awarded in a field, such as a PhD, a JD, or an MD—averages $107,000 annually and usually marries someone else with a terminal degree, doubling the household income. Even if we had financial equity in education today (and we do not), our educational system alone would still consistently engineer racially predictable economic disparities. Yet here we are as Indigenous people, doubling down on this system even though it fundamentally operates against the best interests of our people, has never made us into good, successful white folks, and never will.

I believe in education. I earned a PhD, and I'm glad I did. But the educational system that ignores us and denigrates our existence will not be the source of our liberation. It has to be turned on its head. And some indigenous communities, discussed in greater detail in a later chapter, are doing just that.

Consider the twenty-two Hawaiian-medium (immersion) schools in Hawaii where truancy is not a significant problem. In contrast, the truancy rate at Red Lake Middle School in Minnesota is close to 50 percent every day. Then consider the blockbuster academic achievement data produced by Waadookodaading Ojibwe Language Institute in Reserve, Wisconsin, when their student peers at the tribal school rarely meet the test benchmarks set through the Bureau of Indian Education. Tribal-language learning interrupts truancy, and engages families and communities.

If someone is figuring out what to do about these problems in education, maybe we should pay closer attention to their work. Doing the same thing we've done for the past two hundred years and expecting a different result for the upcoming school year is insane. Language revitalization is innovative and produces results—in English and math as well as the target indigenous language—that everyone can believe in.

Senator Paul Wellstone once said, "We all do better when we all do better."[2] Indigenous language revitalization is one way we can do better. It is how students can reach the finish line with high school and beyond it more consistently. It is also how we become self-sufficient, load-bearing citizens contributing to society instead of being designated wards of the government stuck in cycles of dependency. It is how we break the chains of oppression.

In our own circles, the language is critical for cultural continuity. Most of our ceremonies are conducted exclusively in our tribal languages. To lose the languages is to lose our ceremonial medium, and in many cases the ceremonies themselves. The deepest levels of meaning are the most potent, in everything from medicines to nuanced ceremonial and religious content, and in many cases those levels can only be reached through a living language.

* * *

When I advocate for indigenous language revitalization, I often encounter a quiet form of passive resistance. Many think the language is nice or pretty—like the song of a bird in the forest. There's a sense that the forest and especially humans don't depend on that sound for anything; it doesn't fill bellies or help people lead longer, healthier, happier lives. But nothing could be further from the truth. Physical, mental, and spiritual health are deeply intertwined. There is no way to improve our health without taking a full, holistic approach. We can't stop the bludgeon of forced assimilation. Instead, we need to decolonize and re-indigenize everything we do. This is where real healing will come from. And again, the language is a powerful tool in the arsenal for such an undertaking.

In the 1970s, Bruce Alexander and Simon Fraser conducted a series of experiments on substance abuse now known as Rat Park. In previous studies on substance abuse, scientists put a rat in an empty cage and allowed it to self-inject heroin, morphine, amphetamine, cocaine, and other drugs. The rat would press the injection lever until it died. This showed the powerful addictive and destructive force of the drugs on an individual creature. Alexander and Fraser re-created the experiment, but instead of using an isolated rat, they created a rat park—a large space full of toys, with room to roam and the opportunity to play and reproduce. The rats in the park left the drugs alone. The study suggested that addiction was only partly about the drugs—it was much more about the entire environment drug users find themselves in. Alexander and Fraser offered other examples to back up their claims. During the Vietnam War, 20 percent of those who served used heroin, but less than 3 percent became addicts. Likewise, most people who get pain meds after surgery do not become addicts. The scientists argued that instead of shaming drug users or incarcerating them or even treating them with individual treatment plans, we should be focusing on their entire environment. The more positive hooks we have in someone, the greater the chance that they will stay sober, stay in school, and so forth. I believe that with good intentions, many of the white folks who have created our educational system, our political system, and our shared social fabric forget that what looks like Rat Park for our white citizens might look like an empty cardboard box to our Natives. We need our own versions of Rat Park. We need access to our languages and cultures.

Albert Einstein is attributed with having said, "If you judge a fish by its ability to climb trees, it will spend its whole life believing that it is stupid."[3] We keep making our kids climb trees and judging them for their failures. Even tribally run schools operate with mainstream educational methods, teach a white-dominated curriculum, and hire a predominantly (and sometimes exclusively) white teaching corps. We can put a brown face on assimilation if the school is run by a tribe, but it is assimilation nonetheless. Instead, we need to tell our little ones to swim for the river. Learning one's language is a powerful decolonizing and healing act. It allows our kids to really swim.

Iota Cabral, one of many strong, Native-Hawaiian-language advocates, told me that when his people are pressed to explain why they do what they do, they invoke the concept of mauli, or spiritual fire. The Hawaiians believe that there are three sources of mauli: the head (where the soul resides), the belly button (the connection to one's maternal line), and the genitals (the source of one's future generations). Ancient Hawaiian customs nurtured all of these. I was especially moved by the customs around piko, or the belly button. When a child was about a week old and lost his or her umbilical cord, Hawaiians used to take it out to the lava beds, carve a divot, and place the cord there with a rock on top. Families remembered these places. When a girl grew up and had children of her own, she drew a circle around her divot and placed the umbilical cords of her children in a line next to it. The petroglyphs stunned me—acres and acres of divots and circles, all bonding people to one another through their maternal lines, to Mother Earth, and to their specific part of the planet. So when queried about why the language is important to them, Hawaiians say it's all about mauli—spiritual fire. Well-tended fires grow strong; neglected fires grow weak. Children need to learn their native language so they have strong mauli.

Indigenous language is vitally important for Indigenous people; that should be motivation enough for us as well as the rest of the world to actively support it. But there's more at stake than what's happening in Native communities and our capacity to be good, healthy neighbors and productive citizens. The rest of the world needs our ideas. Everyone needs to heal and interrupt the colonial process, which dehumanizes us all.

* * *

White folks need healing. They are the primary beneficiaries of the systems of oppression operating in the world today. It hurts more to be a victim of oppression than a beneficiary, but oppression dehumanizes everyone.

Humans have been mean to one another the world over since the first of us picked up a club and took a neighbor's food by force. But a special kind of violence evolved in the Middle East and Europe at the dawn of the agricultural age: colonial violence. Instead of just taking someone's resources, this kind of violence overtook whole populations and dictated how they could worship and which languages they could speak. It was an enabling mechanism for slavery and many other manifestations of oppression. Native Americans have endured five hundred years of this kind of violence; white folks have endured thousands of years of it. It is no surprise to me that people in communities of color dominate the crimes of desperation and poverty—drug crimes, burglary, and so forth—because this oppression has made them disproportionately poor. But white men dominate the ranks of school shooters and serial killers because the use of violence to cope with and solve problems is woven into the cultural fabric of white societies. White people need healing too. Their earth-based, indigenous connections have been so thoroughly eroded and colonized that they do not have sufficient cultural resources to lead themselves or anyone else to peace. Indigenous people can help pollinate the world's garden and lead in this direction because we have more than a vestigial remnant of a different way of thinking and doing things. Our tools for doing so are often embedded in our languages.

The extinction of a tree or animal species does not destroy an entire ecosystem yet always alters it. And too many losses can topple everything. The same is true for our shared cultural ecosystems. Linguistic diversity, like biodiversity, is a requirement for health. As humans, we are connected to one another but not entirely interdependent in all realms. Many of us do not see how very important linguistic and cultural diversity is in our small parts of the world.

Today we are witnessing, through globalization and colonization, the proliferation of a few dominant world religions (Christianity, Judaism, Islam) and a few dominant languages (English, Spanish, Chinese). The pressure on smaller religious and linguistic groups is intense, and many will disappear. This will permanently close off whole channels of human thought, culture, and problem-solving. The cultural, religious, and linguistic bottleneck we are heading toward has the dominant groups in constant, polarized conflict. Religious and ethnic strife is obvious across the world. It is inimical to world peace. In America, politicians have picked immigration and language demography as the new battlegrounds in a huge culture war, as some seek to hold up the supremacy of white, Christian, English-speaking worldviews over the growing bodies of people of color who speak languages other than English. This is not a fight we should be engaged in. Instead of fighting over the transfer of power from one group to another, we should seek to transform the nature of power entirely. Instead of squabbling over who will be the oppressor, we should all be working collectively to fight oppression.

*   *   *

I remember the first time I attended precinct caucuses with my father back in 1978, when I was still too young to vote. There were several farmers there caucusing in Norwegian—probably immigrants, or children of immigrants. The scene was fundamentally

American and quintessentially Minnesotan. But today, it would much more likely be considered subversive and un-American, especially if the language used at the caucus wasn't indigenous to northern Europe. A large, diverse country like the United States needs a common set of laws and a few shared values (for instance, killing people is not okay). And beyond that, the colonizing has to stop. Most of the white folk in America forget that their ancestors fled religious oppression and came here so they could worship and speak as they chose, not so they could impose what they brought here on everyone else.

Linguistic and cultural diversity is healthy because having many different languages and cultures forces us to reach out, understand, tolerate, and educate. That makes the world not only a richer place but one that is far more tolerant and likely to enable all of us to get along. Arthur Schlesinger Jr., and others who have claimed that we need to assimilate everyone into some common melting pot, had it wrong. The strength of countries like Canada and the United States is not in their ability to assimilate many different people into one common language and culture, but rather in their ability to tolerate and accept religious, linguistic, and cultural diversity.

WHAT'S IN THE WAY
||||||||||||||||||||||||||||||||||||||||||||||||||||||||||||||||

LANGUAGE REVITALIZATION IS HARD WORK AND FULL OF challenges. A few major world languages are proliferating at the expense of many others. Only one hundred languages in the world are actively and widely taught at colleges and universities. There are still around 6,700 languages spoken worldwide, but 2,500 are endangered. In the United States and Canada, the number of our languages has fallen from 500 precontact to 150 or so today. Of those, only twenty are spoken by children and only four have such a large and vibrant base of speakers that they will definitely be here one hundred years from now. For many who still have native languages to think about revitalizing, future vitality may be possible, but it is not certain. All depends on the depth and breadth of our interventions *today* to save them. That's certainly how I look at my own Ojibwe language.

A language revitalization effort can only be as strong as the language itself. While there are heroic efforts to document Delaware, Wampanoag, Coast Salish, and other highly eroded language groups, these efforts face a steep, uphill climb. For those lucky enough to have truly living languages or, better yet, living languages where intergenerational transmission of the language is still happening, the climb is still steep. But—

to switch metaphors—the more fertile the garden, the easier it is to grow. A language needs humans to speak it, sing it, teach it, and learn it, or surely it will perish.

Colonization has been brutal for every population on the planet. Europeans colonized one another. Irish, Welsh, Basque, and Flemish populations faced incredible pressure on their heritage languages as the English, Spanish, and French empires conquered and colonized them. Those enlarged empires then went on to colonize populations in Africa, Asia, and the Americas. Even when the physical violence used to control human populations abated, other forms of colonization continued. English was required as the language of instruction in all Irish schools, for example, and remained so long after the wars were over. For most linguistically marginalized populations, such colonization has never stopped.

In the United States, more than thirty states now have official English-language policies. This is a recent political trend, in response to increasing Anglo-American angst about the growth of brown, Spanish-speaking populations. But the impact on indigenous languages is also profound—reducing funding opportunities, installing new prohibitions against non-English languages in many schools and organizations, and stigmatizing language enclaves, work, publications, and use.

In 2015, in a restaurant in Coon Rapids, Minnesota, a couple was speaking Swahili to keep their conversation from being understood by their children. A white woman nearby was so angry to hear them using a language other than English that she got up, screamed at them, and smashed her beer mug into the other woman's face. Some restaurants in various places across the country have even reportedly tried to ban altogether people from non-English-speaking linguistic groups. Many times, American citizens have called the Immigration and Customs

Enforcement (ICE) agency or other law enforcement services to report people whom they have heard speaking languages other than English, without even bothering to find out that they are usually American citizens.

Some Americans, fearing that the oppressed are somehow going to flip roles with the oppressors, spend tremendous energy, money, and political power to maintain the current racial and linguistic hierarchy. They pass laws and regulations that make it harder for members of racial minorities to vote and to access voting information in any language other than English; they berate, badger, and call the cops on racial and linguistic minorities; they press for stricter immigration laws and enforcement, regardless of the economic and political consequences; and they weaponize social services to separate children from their families. The damage done includes an increasing hostility to languages other than English. There is lack of support and outright resistance and sometimes persecution.

In her brilliant book, *White Fragility: Why It's So Hard for White People to Talk About Racism*, racial-equity educator Robin DiAngelo wrote about the concept of "white fragility." DiAngelo, herself a white woman, discusses the special barriers that whites face when encountering anything outside of white racial and cultural homogeneity. She notes that while people of color have to leave their communities to navigate a world dominated by whites and routinely experience racial discomfort, whites are highly insulated from that discomfort. They can travel the world, and someone will usually accommodate them by speaking English. Most whites live in communities that are predominantly white, work in spaces that are predominantly white, and have their children educated in such places. They might go to East Los Angeles or an Indian reservation, but they can always leave, and usually do. Any muscles they have that might get exercised by consistent racial discomfort have atrophied. And they have an unreasonably high expectation for being racially and linguistically comfortable. Trying to revitalize an indigenous language, or simply trying to have a conversation in Hmong, Somali, or Spanish, can get a powerful negative reaction from them. White fragility stymies such efforts.

White fragility is experienced by conservative and liberal white folks alike. And many people from both ends of the political spectrum resist meaningful language revitalization. In recent years, growing white nationalism has turned more of that resistance from passive (inertia, lack of support) to active and overt. There is a concerted effort to protect Anglo racial, cultural, religious, and linguistic homogeneity in America especially, but in many other places as well.

*   *   *

Obstacles to successful language revitalization are abundant outside of the target-language communities, but they are just as prolific inside of our own communities. Even where we have power to act in the best interest of our language and culture, we often fail to do it. In the Severn region of Canada, most of the Oji-Cree communities have 100 percent fluency in the tribal language. Some of the Ojibwe communities in northwestern Ontario, like Lac La Croix, also have high fluency rates. Access to many such places requires a boat or floatplane in summer and driving across an ice road in winter. But tribal people there are aware of and connected to the rest of the world. As soon as a road is built into one of these isolated communities, people leave. And often some of the best and brightest leaders find the most demands on their time and expertise outside of their home communities. People in such places want the benefits of modern technology and entertainment. Once there is electricity and a satellite dish, the kids start watching Sponge Bob in English. Even without a residential boarding school overtly oppressing the language community and straining family cohesion, the intergenerational transmission of the tribal language is pressured from the inside. The kids start singing the Sponge Bob songs to one another, then chatting with one another in English, even as they answer their parents in Ojibwe or Oji-Cree. Over time, it takes a powerful toll on the language community. Asking people there not to put up a satellite dish is no more reasonable than asking mainstream Americans to give up access to their modern lifestyle. The water is rushing down the mountain—the change is constant. And most people just go with the flow.

Historical trauma plagues most indigenous populations. All sentient life has a genetic imprint from its experiences. That's what gives humans their fight or flight response and tells the monarch butterflies when and where to migrate. The study of epigenetics has taught us that even one isolated trauma event can leave a genetic imprint that gets passed forward across generations. All humans have trauma somewhere in their family tree. Today, even a person with almost every kind of privilege and advantage in life sometimes experiences an unexplained depression or self-destructive behavior. But for some groups of people—think of blacks who have experience with slavery or Native Americans who have experience with genocide or residential boarding schools—the traumas were especially intense and widespread, and today they don't just pop up occasionally; they pop up like popcorn. The result is that we sometimes disengage or self-destruct in the face of our own healing and betterment. And collectively, we disengage and destroy ourselves and one another in many ways.

This dynamic is further complicated by the fact that we don't just have to deal with historical trauma. We also have to deal with the traps and triggers of learned behavior. Most physical abusers were themselves physically abused. So when the US and Canadian governments took generations of Indigenous children out of their homes and physically abused them, it messed up a lot of people. Many of us figured out how to be healthy, loving parents. But that was in spite of, rather than because of, our schools and governments. Problems related to historical trauma and learned behavior are further compounded by our contemporary trauma. The suicide rate in Indian country is higher than anywhere else in the world. Poverty is endemic in many places. Many of us are at tier one in Abraham Maslow's hierarchy of needs: food, clothing, and shelter. Thinking about higher-order needs like emotional healing, community cohesion, and language revitalization is a lot to ask of people who are trying to figure out where to sleep tonight.

While historical trauma is real and not to be discounted, all too often we talk about this issue in one dimension only. It's not just the bad stuff that gets passed forward; the good stuff gets passed forward too. Those of us who survived the genocide and colonization are the ones who figured out how to get enough food, cooperate, build something, and keep our languages and cultures alive. We are more than the sum of our tragedies.

Most of the speakers of indigenous languages learned their languages in the home. Most grew up in indigenous communities. All grew up in a different time. The tactics and strategies families used to learn and teach do not always work outside of the home, and they almost never work the same way they did in those environments. Revitalizing your language requires a lot of thought and communication. I have frequently heard people say things like, "Writing it down is a waste of time. That's not our way. I never wrote it down when I was a kid." But most of our kids are not growing up hearing the language every day. I've heard people say, "Teaching the language at school is a waste of time. It has to start at home." But most speakers of tribal languages in most places are past the age of having and raising children. If it has to start at home, it will never start. When young, passionate, emerging language warriors want to pick up a modern arsenal to tackle language revitalization, the elders who don't yet see the value of those tools create a big barrier.

Our communities are often rife with oppression dynamics on the inside. Paulo Freire's famous book *Pedagogy of the Oppressed* details the anatomy of oppression. When a group of people is oppressed, the oppression itself gets housed inside of those who are oppressed. The Pilgrims, for example, sailed across the ocean and escaped from their oppressors, but they did not escape oppression. They brought it with them. Safe from their oppressors in a new land, they internalized the oppression, and it manifested itself as blame and shame in their culture. They soon started to oppress one another laterally, and sometimes famously, with the Salem witch trials. And, of course, they oppressed other people—Natives and eventually blacks.

Freire identifies four pillars that prop up any kind of oppression: internal, lateral, intra-oppressed group, and external. Only one comes from the outside. All the others happen inside of the oppressed group. This happens with regard to racial oppression, where antiblack and anti-indigenous views permeate all people, including blacks and Indigenous peoples. It happens in gender dynamics, where women support and defend patriarchy, sometimes without even realizing it. In Native communities, we have a crabs-in-the-bucket pattern. When someone starts to climb out and do something—working for financial betterment, showing political ambition, or sticking their neck out for our language and culture—the other crabs grab him or her by the back legs and pull them back down. This manifests itself in lack of support, gossip, bickering, discouragement, lack of funding, and political attacks on, by, or between folks trying to advance the tribal language.

Most of the generation of Native grandparents went through residential boarding schools. Many of them decided not to teach their Native language to their children in order to protect their kids, fearing it would mark them for persecution. And America's educational system has never been friendly to anyone who doesn't speak English.

I have often heard elders blaming young people for not being willing to learn, and I have heard young people blaming elders for not being willing to teach. We worry so much about being blamed for what is being lost that the assignment of blame gets more energy than the work of getting language development off the ground. This is a lateral oppression dynamic and we need to see it for what it is, name it, and not do it. After all the things our people have been through, we are right where we should be. We are actually in better shape than we should be, because we still have languages to fight for. We all have something to learn. We all have something to teach. We need one another. We need one another's knowledge, commitment, support, and action. Fighting colonization starts with not fighting one another. No blaming. No shaming.

Blaming and shaming have special manifestations in Native communities. We are inundated with negative stereotypes of who we are. Misguided comments from outsiders are sometimes easy to see. But those coming from inside Native communities are hard to ward off. Chimamanda Ngozi Adichie said that the problem with stereotypes is not that they are incorrect so much as they are incomplete. For example, there is a belief that Indians are drunks. That's not true. Native populations actually have a higher percentage of people who abstain from alcohol than most other racial and ethnic groups in America. So that's a stereotype, not a fact. But we also have profound, real problems with abuse of alcohol and other drugs in Native communities, and all the data supports that reality. The truth of substance abuse problems feeds the stereotype, even if the information that feeds the stereotype is incomplete. But the stereotype sticks. You can have three hundred inebriated, white college students in a bar and nobody is going to say that white folks are all drunks. But you can have three hundred inebriated, white college students and one Indian, and someone will think that all Indians are drunks and will often voice the thought. The pervasiveness of this stereotype leaves many young, Native people with a deep feeling of shame. The negative image of the drunken Indian has been internalized.

Throughout Indian country, inside of Native communities, we joke around about poverty, unreliability, and unhealthy food as if those things are the defining features of a Native identity. We talk about Indian cars, meaning beat-up old junkers, with bumpers held on by duct tape and baling wire and tires that are brothers from different marriages. It always gets a good laugh. Many of us have experienced poverty, so we can relate. And almost nobody says that's not us. But that's not us.

Precontact, there wasn't even a concept of abject poverty. There was scarcity and there was abundance. We were not defined by scarcity. We didn't internalize poverty as a marker of authenticity. But we often do now.

We talk about Indian time, as if being late is our way. But anybody who was late was less successful as a hunter, wild rice harvester, trapper, or fisherman. Being late meant watching your kids go hungry. People were not late, back in the day. But we are now. And we hold that up defensively as the Indian way.

Thomas Stillday of Red Lake said that Indian time just means we will sit here and do our ceremony until it's done, with no shortcuts. It's not an excuse to be late or lazy.

Some Indians struggling with these stereotypes feel that claiming a strong Native identity means living in poverty and poor health. Who really wants to do that? So they embrace a modern (predominantly white) American identity and navigate the non-Native world with a different definition of success that often leads them away from their language and culture. And for others, poverty is an inescapable reality. The fact that it's not Native in origin is lost in the pervasiveness of the experience. They own that experience as a defining feature of what it means to be Native, rather than embracing more foundational things like language and culture. Either way, they internalize the stereotypes, which drive people away from revitalizing their language and culture.

Wendell Chino, former tribal chairperson for the Mescalero Apache, said that leading in Indian country is "bullets in the front, arrows in the back." Non-Natives will attack you when you stick your neck out and try to interrupt the system. And revitalizing an indigenous language is an interruption of the system. But the Indians will be just as cruel. If they identify strongly with the status quo, those advocating to change it are a threat. A knowledgeable language keeper may feel threatened by a new writing system or educational structure because it calls for placing authority for language work outside of that person. Tribal politicians may feel threatened because you are proposing your own agenda, not theirs. Anyone who doesn't understand their language and culture can feel threatened by those who place value on something they don't know. Language warriors need super-thick, elephantlike skin to deal with all the attacks. We also have to be aware that most people have paper-thin skin and are hypersensitive to change and disruption. Knowing this is critical to being an effective disruptor.

* * *

Getting a language revitalization effort off the ground is complicated by a lack of quality language resources. I have never met anyone doing this work who says that they have too many books and tools and schools. And when getting something started, the first cohort of leaders has to fill all roles, full time: teachers, administrators, grant writers, curriculum developers, politicians, advocates, and often parents or grandparents. It can be overwhelming, and that discourages engagement, leads to burn-out, and puts too many eggs in too few baskets to sustain such a monumental undertaking.

It takes money to scale up a language revitalization effort. I called Rosetta Stone, the massive, online language-software company, to see if they were interested in doing a program for Ojibwe. They said yes. But they needed a multimillion-dollar investment up front. Some of the money would pay the Ojibwe language folks who would provide material for the program. Some would be used for their proprietary, artificial-intelligence engine, their tech team, their marketing team, and their shareholders. Whether that is reasonable or not is beside the point. If you want to do it, you need the money. The same is true for a school, a collegiate teacher training program, or even a book or website.

Not everyone likes to hear this. But the folks in Indian country who are the most skilled at writing and getting big grants are often not the people who would do the most impactful language work if they got a grant. This means that some of the tribes that are the most depleted in terms of language and the most culturally assimilated are best at playing the government-grants game. Immersion used to be the guiding model for how to run an effective language program. Now it's a buzzword for writing a grant to the Administration for Native Americans.

When a tribal government really backs a language effort over a long period of time, politically and financially, amazing things can be accomplished. But tribes usually have two-year election cycles, and the support comes and goes as if on a pendulum. At the Piegan Institute in Montana, the late Darrell Kipp asked his Blackfeet tribal government for money every year for eight consecutive years, and on the eighth year they got $200. Asking your tribe for money to start or sustain programming is a great idea. Banking on that support is less wise. A tribal council can be a powerful bastion of support, or where great dreams go to die.

In all fairness, tribal leaders work under incredible pressure. Most of our communities have really massive issues related to health, substance abuse, jobs, housing, and poverty. Tribal leaders have to deliver on these things for their people. They often do care about the tribal language, but it's rarely priority number one. I believe that language revitalization can deliver on all of those things. When we heal culturally and spiritually, then physical health follows. Language revitalization is critical to sovereignty. And it creates expansive new employment opportunities.

But not everyone sees it that way. I find it very telling when I visit with Seminole tribal members. The Florida Seminole tribe is one of the most financially successful indigenous nations in the world. They have a huge gaming business, and they also own and operate the Hard Rock Café enterprise and many other national and international businesses. They have eliminated poverty for all tribal members. And their political clout in Florida is beyond question. But if you ask them what keeps

them up at night, they always say that it is language and culture loss. I see our tribal leaders working hard—some with lots
of integrity, some with less—climbing the mountain of economic prosperity and political sovereignty. What I fear is that
the climb will take a long time, and when they finally reach the
summit, they will look around and say, "Oh my God, we just
climbed the wrong mountain. We should have been climbing
the mountain of language and culture revitalization while we
still had a chance."

* * *

Language revitalization is hard work. It can consume every
waking minute of a person's life. It's exhausting. Done right, it
saturates your time and energy, and a lot of people aren't ready
for that. It can be isolating. Human beings have only so many
hours in a day, and if something else gets shoved onto our
plates, something else necessarily falls off. There is an opportunity cost for everything we say yes to. Keeping language at
the center requires constant dedication and prioritization.

Many of our people who really care about the language are
struggling in varying degrees with everything else life throws
at us. Relationships, finances, parenting, grandparenting, and
gainful employment also take time and attention. And dealing
with a friend or relative who is struggling with health, mental
health, or substance abuse can distract or even derail anybody's
train.

We are still battling gigantic structures of systemic racism
and oppression. Over 30 percent of Native kids are still adopted
or fostered out of our homes and communities, even after
passage of the Indian Child Welfare Act. Those kids are rarely
raised in a Native community, much less a Native language
community. We are still occupied, still being colonized. This

happens in public schools. This happens as we are socialized in mainstream America, where we voluntarily immerse ourselves in foreign (English) language and culture. Even when tribes control schools, community functions, and politics, we often become agents of our own oppression as we put a brown face on assimilation but make it assimilation nonetheless.

This is starting to change. Increasingly, more liberated and indigenous ideologies are starting to infiltrate our new political order. More tribes are adopting food sovereignty programs and see emerging tribal support for cultural efforts. But we have already seen much damage to the health and prioritization of our languages. More Natives spend their energy redefining indigeneity than they do working to keep our languages and cultures alive. Language loss is self-perpetuating. All that's necessary for most languages to die is for us to do too little or nothing.

HOW I DID IT
||||||||||||||||||||||||||||||||||||||||||||||

Learning Ojibwe as a Second Language

IF EVERYONE WAITED TO HAVE CHILDREN UNTIL THEY WERE emotionally, physically, and financially ready, humans would not reproduce. Parents always start this job with more questions than answers—that's the challenge and beauty of parenthood. We parents enter the endeavor knowing that the job will not be comfortable. By expecting hard work, we are actually better able to lean into it. After all, disappointment is inversely proportional to expectations. When you fall in love with your child, the problems and stresses seem much smaller. You embrace even the most daunting and unpleasant parts of the job with a motivation unimaginable for those who have never had the experience. All of a sudden, this new relationship that has existed for all of one minute has eclipsed all others. You could jump in front of a moving train if your baby needed that. Puke, fevers, sleep deprivation—these onerous challenges become mere badges of honor and sources of entertainment. Falling in love is a powerful motivator.

My secret to successfully learning my tribal language as a second language is the same as my secret for raising my nine children—I fell in love. Falling in love with your language is every bit as powerful a motivator. Just as we need to take a

45

minute to really look at, smell, and hold our babies when they are born, we need to do the same for our languages. Fall in love. You'll figure the rest out.

* * *

Like many great love stories, mine happened by accident. By the time I finished high school, I was determined to get out of my hometown—Bemidji, in northern Minnesota—and never come back. I think many high schoolers have some version of this idea when they are eighteen. But mine was fueled by some really painful experiences with overt and sometimes physically violent racism, directed at me. I thought that going to college at Princeton University, over a thousand miles away from home, would enable me to escape from racial tension and misunderstanding. And I wasn't just running from that unpleasantness. I was running from myself too. I was so stigmatized and bullied that I thought a fresh start in a fresh place with few Native Americans would enable me to pass for something else. If I could pass as Latinx, Arab, Filipino, or Greek, then I wouldn't be doubted or attacked or stereotyped, or at least not as painfully. I was naïve, to say the least.

I grew fast when I went to college. Racial tension followed me there, but it changed. Yes, people asked me where my tomahawk was and told me that Indians couldn't handle their liquor. But I didn't usually feel unsafe or oppressed. And even though I was running from things, I was running *toward* things too. I learned a great deal academically, but even more outside the classroom. The friends I made there remain some of my greatest friends yet today. We see each other regularly. They supported me. But they challenged me too, with fundamental questions like, "What makes you Indian?" Those questions sent me soul-searching.

I started to think deeply about identity. Having Native blood mattered. Most Spanish-speaking people in North and South America have Native blood, and plenty of people who identify as white or black Americans have some Native blood too. Surely that blood mattered. But what mattered most? What distinguished and defined a person as indigenous, predominantly indigenous, or indigenous and something else? I thought about peer acceptance, community, connection. Then I started to really think about culture and language. A Chinese American is different from someone who is simply Chinese. The differences are not biological, and they are more than a distinction of nationality or citizensaip; they are cultural too. And although there are plenty of Chinese Americans who speak Chinese, there are plenty who don't. But someone who is Chinese speaks at least one of the languages of China, and that further defines them. It had to be this way for all people. I felt Ojibwe. But I didn't speak Ojibwe.

I started flying home for cultural functions and spending more of my summers going to ceremonies, tending fire for my mother's sweat lodge, visiting elders, asking questions, and eventually trying to tune in to our language. I bought books and attended Ojibwe language tables. I brought any portable resources I found back to New Jersey for the academic year at Princeton. For my senior thesis, I spent a spring and summer in 1990 going to boat landings and interviewing people during the treaty-rights dispute in Wisconsin. The experience heightened my understanding of historical injustice, racism, and the importance of indigenous land tenure, culture, and language.

I studied at the Woodrow Wilson School of Public and International Affairs at Princeton, thinking I would later pursue a law degree and maybe even enter politics. But I soon became disillusioned with that idea and knew that even if I was smart enough to be a good lawyer, I would never be a happy one. When I finished college, to the horror of my parents, I decided not to get a job, not to go to graduate school, not to do Peace Corps, Teach for America, or anything like any of my ambitious classmates. I was coming home. My plan was to walk the earth—to learn my language, to get initiated into the Medicine Dance (the primary religious society of the Ojibwe), to go fasting, hunting, and searching for meaning in the very place I swore I would never return to when I first left. I'm not even sure if my parents were pleased to have me home. They warned me that I would receive no financial support of any kind from them and seemed to assume that hunger or the desire to take a woman out on a date would eventually motivate me to get a job or do something with my life. But they were watching me from a distance. This was a formative time and everyone close to me knew it.

I was excited and determined to embark on a path of self-discovery, but I didn't have much of a plan. I just knew I wanted to learn from the best, and as far as I could tell, the best was Archie Mosay. He was an elder from the St. Croix Reservation in Wisconsin. His village, Balsam Lake, is 245 miles from Bemidji, but just an hour and a half from the Twin Cities, and it thrummed with motor vehicles, farms, businesses, and tourists. It seemed like an unlikely place to find what I was looking for.

Although Balsam Lake isn't geographically far from the Twin Cities, in a cultural sense, it could not have been any further away. Archie was born in 1901, which meant he was just a year too young to serve in World War I—and too old to serve in World War II. His namesakes were veterans from the US Civil War. He was an adult the first time he saw a black man or a car. He was a teenager when he got the name Archie—a "gift" from the white farmer who hired him as a field hand

and couldn't pronounce his Native name, *Niibaa-giizhig* (Evening Sky). His English was a little clunky, but his Ojibwe was truly eloquent. Archie had served as Oshkaabewis (Messenger) in the Medicine Dance from age twelve to age seventy, when his father died. His knowledge of that ceremony was superlative. He had been serving as chief of the lodge for a couple decades by 1991, when I went to see him.

I drove the 245 miles from my house to his because of his reputation as a spiritual leader and because I knew that he did his ceremonies the old way—no shortcuts, a full two-week initiation rite, and no English. I was both self-assured and incredibly naïve when I hunted him down. This was before cell phones, so when I got to Balsam Lake, I started looking up Mosays in the phone book. The first one I called was his son Dan, who gave me a thorough interrogation and then finally directions to his dad's house. In spite of Archie's late and slow entry into the modern world, when I met him he was home alone, scraping down sticks to make tobacco out of red willow bark and watching *WWF SummerSlam* on a color television.

I knew to bring tobacco and gifts. I still remember carrying in the venison sausage and a yard each of red and yellow cloth. He gave me a hard look. I couldn't tell if it was because I was a stranger and not to be trusted or he was just old and it was taking him a little while to process an unexpected arrival. He turned off the television and then did the strangest thing. His voice was especially deep—a second bass if he were to sing in a modern choir. He shook my hand, looked me straight in the eye, and said, "I've been waiting for you."

I thought he might have had me confused with someone else. After all, he didn't even know my name or anything about me. But he explained that he had a dream about a young man who would come to see him, someone who was destined to do something important for the people, and that he had to teach him. He said that young man was me.

I didn't know what to think or say. He offered me a chair and asked if I would stay for a while. I spent much of that summer at his house. Most of the time I drove him around to various ceremonies and powwows, helped fill pipes, set up food, ate, and visited. Sometimes I skinned animals so the hides could be used for ceremony. Sometimes I read books or chatted while he bent snuff-can lids into jingles for jingle dresses. I drove him to the bank to cash the small pension check he received from Polk County for his years driving trucks and snowplows. He couldn't even endorse the check, but I was more convinced than ever that he was the best-educated man I had ever met. I listened a lot, and he always engaged me in Ojibwe first, even though I had limited understanding in those early years.

I had managed to save a couple thousand dollars from my construction job while in college and from graduation gifts. I stretched that money as thin as I could. But Indians in general, and ceremony people in particular, were really generous. People were always coming to Archie's house for namings and other ceremonies, and they always brought food. Archie wouldn't accept rent money from me. I was able to stay in this position for a long time.

He told me that the language was the key to everything in our culture. It was the cipher for sacred knowledge and the Ojibwe way of being. All I really wanted to do was stay with Archie after that and learn his secrets. But I also knew that I had to use all tools available to accelerate my learning. I wouldn't have many years with Archie, who was already more than ninety years old. At our first meeting, I passed tobacco to him to ask to be initiated into the Medicine Dance, but the initiation wouldn't be until the following summer. So I went home to rural Bemidji to sew blankets, make tobacco, hunt and fish for food offerings, and pick up more tools for my quest.

I stayed in constant contact with Archie, usually through his daughter Dora Ammann, who remains one of my greatest friends and mentors today. At the same time, I sought out Earl Nyholm (who has since changed his name to Earl Otchingwan-igan). Earl was a professor of Ojibwe at Bemidji State University, the first collegiate Ojibwe language program in the world. He had a great reputation in the language world as a coauthor of what would become the most widely used dictionary for the language. Even more important, he lived and worked where I was based. I wanted to honor Archie's request that I pick up the language, and Earl seemed like the perfect teacher. This had the potential to feed my intellectual underpinnings too. I was highly motivated.

Archie usually gave me a kick to get going. But Earl usually slowed me down. Confusing though those mixed messages were, I think in the long run they helped me stay driven and persistent on the one hand, and patient on the other. With language work, that made for powerful medicine.

I found Earl, signed up for classes, and immediately started to pester him about my language and culture quest. I made an appointment to get started. I arrived at the agreed-upon time to find him sitting at a table, writing something on a piece of note paper. He was looking out the window and didn't even appear to notice me. He crumpled up the paper and wrote something down again. Earl was slow and deliberate. It could be forty degrees below zero with a howling northwest wind, and he would walk unbearably slowly, saying, "I wasn't born in a hurry-up time." Waiting for him to scribble his note took about twenty minutes. I was filled with stress and frustration. Then he turned to face me and said, "Learn this. Come back. Then we can start." For all my planning and waiting, I had received these three sentences in English and a piece of paper with two sentences in Ojibwe. The paper read, "Weweni gibi-naazikoon gegoo ji-gagwejiminaan sa noongom. Gimiinin asemaa." Translation: "I come to you today with all respect to ask you something. I am giving you tobacco."

I had that line memorized before I even made it back to my car. It took me two more weeks before I could pin him down again for a one-on-one. And I started with the line he taught me and a pipeful of tobacco. He said, "Okay. We can get started." And we did.

I was the most ridiculous student of Ojibwe, and it must have made me maddening company for anyone who knew me. I attended every class and language table I could—Earl's especially, but also Tom White's in Cass Lake, and others. Every night I took all my notes and typed them up, using the opportunity to more deeply process anything someone showed me. I kept scores of notebooks and binders with handwritten and typed notes, and multiple versions of stories and word lists. I typed labels and put them on everything in the house—doors, windows, mirrors, salt and pepper shakers. I even put labels on everything in my parents' kitchen. If they minded, they didn't dare tell me.

My financial plan after college was not much of one, so several months into "walking the earth," I ran out of money. I got a job at Bemidji State University doing recruitment and retention work with Native students. It kept me close to Earl and in the language classes and allowed me to keep doing what I was doing. It enabled my quest, even though it didn't quite feel like a career to me. I started to use Ojibwe for everything I could, and that meant looking for more places to use Ojibwe. There were no immersion schools or language nests (sanctuaries where the tribal language occupied all the airspace). I had to make my own. I had to spend time with Native speakers.

Throughout Minnesota, there was about 100 percent fluency in Ojibwe before World War II. I have rarely met anyone from the Greatest Generation (people born between 1901 and 1927) who grew up in an Ojibwe community in Minnesota who was not a speaker. But the effects of residential boarding schools, urbanization, and other types of assimilation dramatically interrupted the intergenerational transmission of our tribal language (as they did for many other languages). Ojibwe kids had been forced to attend residential boarding schools since the late 1800s, but by World War II, the effects of this and other policies really started to stack up. While most Ojibwe members of the Greatest Generation are speakers, most people born after that are not. By the early 1990s, only the elders, most of whom had been born during World War I or the Great Depression, were first speakers of Ojibwe. So I sought them out.

Scott Headbird and his wife, Susie, lived just a couple miles from my parents' house on Mission Road, west of Cass Lake. Their place was tiny and rustic, and Susie's knickknacks and owl figurines adorned every windowsill and every inch of wall space. On my first visit, I was nervous. Scott was lean and leathery, sitting at his kitchen table wearing thick-rimmed Indian Health Service glasses and a red baseball hat with a stiff brim tilted to one side. I fumbled around for my pouch of tobacco and used the lines Earl had taught me: "Weweni gibi-naazikoon gegoo ji-gagwejiminaan sa noongom. Gimiinin asemaa." I handed him a pipeful of the tobacco. And I followed up with, "Niwii-nanda-gikendaan gidinwewininaan," meaning, "I want to learn our language."

Scott stared at me for what seemed like an eternity, as if he

couldn't believe what he had just heard. He didn't smile. He
didn't respond. I was certain that I had bumbled the exchange—
said something wrong or offensive. He stood straight up and
left. I sat alone at his kitchen table, unsure of what to do next.
I could hear him rummaging around in the bedroom, and I
started to wonder if he might be loading a shotgun. But I stayed.
A few minutes later, he came out with his own pouch of tobacco,
saying, "Miigwech gii-pi-izhaayan omaa ji-nanda-gikendaman
gidinwewininaan. Geget giga-wiidookoon." Translation: "Thank
you for coming here to learn our language. I will definitely help
you." Then he handed me tobacco, saying, "ji-mikwendaman
waandamoonaan," meaning, "so you remember what I tell you."
And we got started.

My experiences with Archie, Earl, Scott, and others demonstrated the power of tobacco in the Ojibwe world. Learning the
language was not just an academic enterprise; it was a cultural
and spiritual quest. And it required a cultural and spiritual
approach. That meant prayer and protocol, not just flash cards
and study sessions.

* * *

There is no way to separate a language from its culture, so I
took an immersive approach to both. I don't just mean looking
for a place where I could hear Ojibwe. I did do that. But I did
more. Ojibwe spaces are constantly penetrated and permeated
by non-Native language, ways of thinking, and material goods.
I wanted, to the highest degree possible in this day and age, to
go deeper.

As I continued to grow the list of first speakers I regularly visited and pestered in Ojibwe, continued to prepare for my initiation into the Medicine Dance with Archie, and eagerly applied
myself to Earl's academic instruction, I also went back to basics

by developing my personal spiritual practice. I was really just trying to get centered in my world. I had no idea it could take me anywhere other than the woods at home. But it did.

Archie, in addition to running Medicine Dance, was a ceremonial drum chief and officiated at countless naming ceremonies and other cultural events. In the Ojibwe world, we believe in a common creator for all life of every kind, but we also believe that the Great Spirit made other manidoog (spirits) and placed them among us. It's kind of like what happens when someone becomes a parent—the parent comes first, but the kids can grow up, become forces in their own right, and even advise the parent. So when we pray, we invoke our creator, but also these other spirits all around us—spirits in each of the four winds, the water, and many others. I sat with Archie and went through the spirits he routinely talked to for these ceremonies. And then I listened to how he talked to and about each of them when he was officiating. I went back to Earl and showered him with questions to make sure I was catching the complex grammatical patterns and nuances Archie used.

Then every morning I got up early and, no matter how windy, rainy, or cold, I stood outside in the same spot and offered tobacco. I just held it in my hand, looking out at the little pond in front of my house, surrounded by the trees my father had planted all those years before. I really took my time. I spoke out loud, all by myself. I tried to be as thorough as possible. I really focused on directing my prayerful thought to making the world a better place. I watched the flickers come back in the spring, listened to the redwing blackbirds' lazy trill in the summer, smelled the musty leaves and pine needles in full splendor in the fall, and reveled in the harsh winter air. Archie had cautioned me to be careful about what I asked for. Sometimes if someone asked for strength they got a horrible test that forced them to do a lot of heavy emotional lifting. Prayer granted, but at what cost? I didn't pray for a specific result. I asked the spirits to show me what I was meant to do. I asked them to help me do good work for them and to best help others. I often gave them thanks for the many blessings in my life.

I spent about thirty minutes every morning in my prayer space. The ground was worn bare throughout every season. And as I traveled, I took that custom with me everywhere I went. I drove a good friend of mine, Tom Goldtooth, to Sun Dance ceremonies at Pine Ridge and Standing Rock. My path was focused on Ojibwe ceremonies, even though I have some Dakota blood running through my veins (and many other kinds too). But I had great respect for Dakota and Lakota ways. I participated in sweat lodge ceremonies there, and I gave offerings at the tree even though I never was a sun dancer. I was always focused on not just my language and culture development, but that of all Ojibwe people.

I went fasting in the spring. It was quite an experience. The substance of what happened to me spiritually there is between me and the manidoog, the spirits. But it was a transformative experience. In the Ojibwe custom, someone who is fasting gives up food and water and also the company of other people. Without the constant thrum and chatter of human activity, I found a test of my courage but also a deeper connection to everything else in the woods. And I started to feel more okay in my own skin than I had ever been before. Earl came once each day to check on me, and I could tell that after seven days, even he was getting ready to pull me down from my fasting platform himself if something didn't give. But something did give, and I emerged from that experience with a sense of purpose and knowledge of self that still drives me today, decades later.

Our family had made maple syrup and sugar every spring of

my life. But spring was a busy time at college, and it had been a few years since I was part of the work crew. I approached the activities with a new lens, as I did with hunting and fishing. The stories I heard as a young boy about the origin of the maple harvest and the substance of a first-kill feast took on new and deeper meaning. I marveled at how much cultural wealth the Ojibwe had preserved. In spite of five hundred really hard years, we still had so much.

Cultural customs both reflect and shape the values of a people. When someone kills his or her first deer, we have a feast where one of the guardians for the successful hunter ritually feeds him. Most of the boys and girls in our family are avid hunters, and all of us went through this ceremony. The hunter has to refuse the first three bites of food, each time giving a reason: "No. I am thinking of children who don't have enough to eat. . . . No. I am thinking of my elders who can't get into the woods to hunt for themselves. . . . No. I'm thinking of my family and the people who came here today to support me." On the fourth offering the hunter can eat. And then he is told that his life has changed. Before this day he was a dependent, but today he provides for everyone. That's what it means to be an adult. And from this day on, he will always have a special power—the power to gather resources. He will have that power when hunting, fishing, and gathering and even when getting a job. The power has to be used to take care of children, elders, family, and community.

Although boys and girls both hunt and go through this ceremony, there are special teachings we give boys about manhood at first-kill feasts. Often, someone talks about the four kinds of deer—fawns, does, young bucks, and mature bucks. The kind of deer most likely to charge a human is not a mature buck, but a young one. The older males have survived a few hunting seasons and lots of predators. They think before they move. The young bucks are full of pheromones and often act more aggressively. They are the most dangerous—and also the most likely to get shot. This teaching about the different types of deer is a metaphor for manhood. Men are most likely to make mistakes when they are young, when they act aggressively. The teachings and guidance that flow from this metaphor is really quite formative.

We had first-kill feasts for my younger brothers during this phase of my life. In addition to the beauties of the ceremony itself, I was reflecting on something my namesake, Mary Roberts, had told me. She said that any time I learned something—a medicine, a song, a ceremony—I had to teach it to at least four other people. I was learning much and was perhaps a little self-absorbed with the effort—just thinking about what I wanted to know and who I wanted to connect with. I was generous with my time and truly helpful to my elders. But I was just now starting to think about what it would mean to honor Mary's teaching, to give everything I learned to at least four other people.

Girls in our family have a special ceremony marking the end of their first year transitioning into womanhood (a year after their first menstrual period). At my sister Megan's coming-of-age feast, I watched her aunties, grandmas, and female namesakes give her teachings. She was wearing a beautiful, white ceremony dress, excited about her transition to adulthood. And she was accepted by these women. One said, "When you see a bunch of women sitting around visiting, come sit with us. You are one of us." Another said, "You have a right and a responsibility to be respected by men. Here is what that means: nobody can hit you or call you names or make you do something sexually that you don't want to do."

I thought about all my previous ambitions—education, law school, politics. And I thought about the ambitions of so many Native people—tribal sovereignty and economic development. We were just embracing non-Native aspirations, tools, ways to solve problems, and ways of relating to one another. It was nauseating. It's not that being financially fit or politically empowered wasn't a good thing; it's that using non-Native ways of doing it obliterated everything else. Using materialism, competition, and individualism was corrosive to the fabric of our indigeneity. What I saw in our cultural toolbox—collaboration, consensus, community—was being invalidated. It reaffirmed my desire to pursue our language and culture. But it also left me searching for a way to integrate these ambitions with navigating the rest of the world from which I could not escape.

That summer, with a full three months off from my new job, I returned to Archie for my initiation into the Medicine Dance. I already had enough intensive language work to follow along better with the long legends and complicated songs. I cried when they hit the drum the first time. I sat in the wigwam every second Archie was in session. I followed the Messengers around as far as they would let me. I started to dream in Ojibwe.

My mother came to Medicine Dance at the end of the ceremony to support me. We camped on the ceremony grounds and cooked meat on a stick, visiting late into the night. I think she was genuinely thrilled to see me so excited about our ways. And she was also genuinely impressed with Archie and his way of doing this ceremony. He gave her tobacco and a blanket and said, "Get your son back here. We need him." I was still overwhelmed by the faith he had in me.

During the second session of lodge (in August), with my initiation complete, I was able to help. It was the only time

I was able to serve as a regular lodge member. I was pushed into leadership work every time afterward. I almost got fired from my new job because the length of the session kept getting extended. All my vacation days were exhausted, and the university was bringing in its new students. If it had come down to it, I would have accepted getting fired as a better consequence than missing a day of the ceremony.

For most of my life, every one of my teachers wanted to teach me about white-guy stuff—history, mathematics, English. There are Native topics and Native ways to approach all academic disciplines too, but they were never centered or valued. I had studied everyone and everything else for so long, it was still revelatory at this point in my journey that I could or should study myself and my own people. It was at odds with everything I had been taught before. But I was getting wiser by the day.

I decided to get even more intentional and systematic about my approach to language and culture. I kept up with the language classes, typing notes, labeling the house, and burning up cars visiting elders.

During one of my visits with Archie, an old Ho-Chunk (Winnebago) man came to visit. His name was Jim Funmaker. He brought in two garbage bags full of tobacco. The Ho-Chunk cultivate their own indigenous seed tobacco. There is a ceremony for its planting, nurturing, and harvesting. Archie traded him even, turning over to him two garbage bags full of red willow tobacco. They both sat there in his kitchen and mixed them together. The mixture is what we call geniginig (mix), and where the word *kinnickinnick* comes from. I went home and spent hours making my own tobacco. I remember a few years later when Jim came to the funeral for Mary Sutton at

Lac Courte Oreilles, and in a high, loud, raspy voice hollered, "What? What? Look at that tobacco. That's white man tobacco. They bought it in a store. I can tell. Hey you, do you smoke the white man tobacco? That's why you're so dizzy all the time. Too much chemical. I don't smoke the white man tobacco. I grow my own tobacco. My leaves are this high."

I continued with Archie's holistic approach to my real Indian education, and with Earl's more academic style. I formed deep relationships with many elders from Ponemah on the Red Lake Reservation, especially Thomas Stillday, Anna Gibbs, and Collins Oakgrove. My ancestral village of Bena is on the Leech Lake Reservation, even though our family property was west of Cass Lake. So I regularly hunted down Leech Lake elders, especially Porky White, Hartley White, Scott Headbird, Susan Jackson, Mark Wakanabo, and Emma Fisher. I was in White Earth often too, especially at the house of Joe Auginaush.

Summertime was lodge time, and that was my primary occupation. During the school year, I went to drum ceremonies most every weekend and soon became good friends with Melvin Eagle and Jim Clark in Mille Lacs. Melvin and I were seated as Messengers on the first ceremonial drum at White Earth together, and he coached me on ceremonial drum talks and etiquette.

I was growing and growing, but I still saw myself as a very inadequate student. I decided to go to graduate school, but instead of linguistics, I chose history, and enrolled at the University of Minnesota. I wanted to use Ojibwe to do oral history of the Ojibwe. I didn't think I'd have to fight for the right to do it, but I did. One of my advisors told me that I shouldn't do oral history and that I shouldn't even study the Ojibwe because I might be biased since I am Ojibwe. I told him, "Is this a serious line of inquiry? Coming from a white man who published twenty books on white men?" He backed off, and I pressed ahead.

I repeatedly returned to all my elder connections, now with a tape recorder to collect their personal reminiscences, historical narratives, and legends. I was developing quite an archive as I spent countless hours trying to transcribe the stories and translate them. At first, this was all done to mine historical information. But eventually Earl asked me to take over as editor of the *Oshkaabewis Native Journal,* the only academic journal of the Ojibwe language. He said he would help proofread material but that he wanted me to assume leadership as editor and to push my own stories into print. It seemed ludicrous to me. I hadn't even finished grad school yet. But after all he had done for me, there didn't seem to be any gracious way to decline. The detailed work with those texts also really expanded my knowledge of the language. And I benefitted from Earl's perfectionism and high-level knowledge of Ojibwe—though all mistakes in any story in that journal are mine.

* * *

My learning was expanding exponentially, and I couldn't see anything to change that trajectory. But that was just my naïveté speaking. In ways both good and bad, everything would churn and change, over and over again.

I fell in love with a beautiful young woman from White Earth, and we soon had a child on the way. I had been working with Archie and Earl for five years by the time my daughter was born. I asked Archie about every detail of preparation for a traditional Ojibwe birth. We drove out into the back roads and fields of northwestern Wisconsin to hunt for medicine. Namewashk. All he knew was the Ojibwe name. I demonstrated the

‖‖‖

full breadth of my ignorance as I picked every form of vegetation imaginable, trying to match his description of a plant with a purple flower, straight stem, and almond-shaped leaves with slightly jagged edges. Not thistle. Not mint. Not clover. There were so many plants with purple flowers. But eventually I found it. He had a good laugh, but I had the medicine for my daughter's first bath and a heart full of hope as we stopped at the Dairy Queen in St. Croix Falls on the way back to Balsam Lake.

I talked to my baby in Ojibwe while she was in utero. I sang songs. It was a beautiful anticipation. But nothing could compare to the reality of her arrival and being in this world. I have cried many times in my life, but usually in pain or loss. Never like this. Uncontrollable tears of joy. It was overwhelming.

I had the medicine ready. No nurses were going to give my child her first bath. I combed the vernix out of her hair and used the medicine, cooked into a warm tea, to wash her body. She looked right at me the whole time, as if she had known me for centuries. I made sure the first words she heard were in Ojibwe. I was all in.

Archie said that we should have a feast four days after her birth to welcome the arrival of a new spirit into the world. Madeline was born in Bemidji and Archie was 245 miles away, so I passed tobacco to Earl to speak for her first feast. It was the middle of winter, and it took a little work for me to bury her placenta by a maple tree—the tree of life. I prepped a traditional game feed. And we waited.

Then came a test. Earl didn't show. The feast had to be on the fourth day after birth and had to be while the sun was up. I had never officiated at any ceremony before. I was just an eager student. But there was no avoiding it without changing the protocol for the feast. So I filled my pipe and spoke for my daughter's first feast. I had no idea then, but it would be the first of many newborn baby feasts in my life and the first of many, many ceremonies that I would officiate. Today I have nine children, three grandchildren, numerous nieces, nephews, and little cousins, and extended family. I have spoken for most of their fourth-day feasts now.

A few months later, I drove my daughter down to Balsam Lake with lots of family in tow and Archie performed her naming ceremony. We had a great lineup of knowledgeable namesakes for my girl. Archie was first, but his daughter Dora Ammann, Veronica Hvezda, and Dennis Jones also pledged to be Madeline's namesakes. They each talked and took a spiritual gift—a dream, a vision—and put it into her. Archie named her Giizhigookwe (Sky Woman).

I didn't think it would be possible to get more motivated. But how could I raise my child in this world if I didn't work to fill her world with every gift and opportunity to know who she was? I still have the recordings of her speaking Ojibwe as a child. I took her everywhere. In Sault Ste. Marie at age two, she was literally running in circles around me as I stood at the podium and delivered a keynote address in Ojibwe to a thousand language activists and teachers. I was nervous. And then she yelled, "Ingii-poogid," meaning, "I farted." The microphone caught the sound and blasted it through the amphitheater, and the entire place erupted into uncontrolled laughing. They couldn't and wouldn't hear anything else I had to say for the rest of the day. But it made the biggest possible impression. Giizhigookwe was famous. The baby who spoke Ojibwe. I was so proud.

Now I had a partner to learn with and teach. I had a reason beyond anything I had encountered before. I realized that my primary goal with the language was to honor my namesake's advice—to teach at least four others, to keep things going, to become replaceable. If I could leave what I learned behind when my time came, I would be a success.

* * *

Like many things in life, my language journey came with triumph and heartache, setbacks and breakthroughs, hope and disillusionment. My first big test came when Archie died. I was only twenty-six years old. Margaret Porter, another Ojibwe speaker from Red Lake and a family friend, gave me the news. The moccasin telegraph traveled faster than Dora Ammann, who called me next with funeral arrangements.

I really only had about five years serving as Archie's Messenger in the lodge. I worked unbelievably hard and hung on his every word. I was in an expansive, growing space spiritually, emotionally, linguistically. But he always did the talks. I was his first student to help him sing. That seems bizarre to me, but he was so great at what he did that nobody else dared take any airtime. Too many eggs in too few baskets. The funeral was huge, with newspapers estimating two thousand people in attendance. There was a man there who, a few years before, had come through ceremony with us, brought in on a stretcher with a life expectancy of just a few more months. Seeing him these years later, walking up to the casket to pay his respects, was a powerful testimony to the power of Archie's mission and impact.

At Dora's request, I had first driven to Ponemah, on the Red Lake Reservation, where I picked up Thomas Stillday to be head officiant, his grandson, Dodgie Natewa, and another language warrior named Isadore Toulouse. As I drove them all to Balsam Lake, my heart was heavy with the loss. But the Ojibwe always have a crazy guffaw and lots of food, even in the most painful moments, and it felt good to be around all of our ceremony people. I was nervous too. Archie was a keeper of lots of rare music, some songs only used once a year, if that. Given his status and degree in the lodge, some of that was required protocol. I was the only likely candidate to be able to speak about, and sing the songs required for, his send-off.

I remember Dora craning her neck to listen as I gave the required talks for the songs, eager and unsure if she would ever really hear them again. I remember Harold Frogg, a deeply respected elder from Lac Courte Oreilles and one of the Chosin Few (from a famous battle in the Korean War), give me a reassuring nod and then put his head down so as to avoid making me feel self-conscious. I had to look away from all the people, the drum chiefs from all over Wisconsin and Minnesota, hundreds of speakers of Ojibwe. I just looked at Archie and sang to him. And the songs came. For me, I had honored my teacher, and that's all I was trying to do. For Dora and Archie's other children, it meant his songs would live. They had plans for me.

When Archie's father had died at the age of 102, back in 1971, Archie was seventy years old and had only been a Messenger in the lodge. In spite of his many decades of apprenticeship, at that age he still felt unworthy and unready to run the lodge by himself. It was quite a testament to his humility. So even though he had been a Messenger in Balsam Lake and lived in Balsam Lake, he first started to officiate that ceremony in Round Lake—the adjacent community on the same reservation and the place where I went for my initiation into the lodge. He did that because John Stone and Henry Merrill, who were colleagues of his, agreed to work with him there and he felt best with all of them co-officiating. He had stayed there for more than twenty years, even after John and Henry died. But it had always been his dream to return to Balsam Lake and do that ceremony where his father had. I went to Round Lake for my lodge initiation because that's where Archie officiated. The following year, he moved his lodge back to Balsam Lake, and I had started to serve as Archie's Messenger.

After Archie's death, his children wanted me to step up and keep things going at Balsam Lake. But I was only twenty-six years old. I knew something, but I had much to learn. I wasn't from Balsam Lake. I didn't want my age or residency in a different community to discourage anyone from attending. And I was scared of messing things up. So I told Dora and her siblings that we should approach Jumbo Wake-Me-Up, Henry Merrill's stepson, and ask him to step up, with our support and assistance. Jumbo agreed, but only if we did it in his home community at Round Lake. It was disappointing for Archie's children, and we had growing pains at first, as Jumbo struggled with leadership dynamics in spite of a great knowledge of the ceremony. But we made it work.

Then Jumbo was involved in a car accident and got a traumatic brain injury, permanently blunting his ability to do the talks. So I ended up doing a lot of his job for him. I was still a Messenger, an understudy, but in reality, I was already doing a lot of the work. He died a few years later, and then one of Archie's sons, Wayne Mosay, worked with me to keep things going. But he passed away a few years after that, and I have been chief of the lodge there ever since.

My first time to a drum ceremony after Archie died put me on the spot. One of Archie's daughters, Betsy Schultz, asked me to speak for numerous bowls of food laid out on the dance hall floor. She put a pouch of tobacco between each of my fingers on both hands and six more in my palms, fourteen in all. Each was for a different person asking for healing from the drum. Betsy didn't break me in easily. She said, "I'm only telling you their names and requests once. I will be listening. Archie never forgot an Indian name." I was sweating quite obviously, but I pulled it off. There was no going back.

All I really wanted to do was study the language. I never thought I would formally teach it, even though I was already working to give my daughter anything I knew. I finished grad school in history and took a job in Milwaukee as a professor of history, but I spent all my time going to northern Wisconsin or back to Minnesota.

I became especially close friends with Thomas Stillday and Anna Gibbs at Ponemah, Melvin Eagle and Jim Clark at Mille Lacs, and many other elders. I deferred to their knowledge and expertise even as I unavoidably had to do more work with the language in a ceremonial context. They are all gone now. Over the next twenty years I lost and buried over fifty elder friends, ceremonial companions, and language warriors. It was hard.

I learned the hard way, too, that there were a lot of ways to experience loss. When I was working in Milwaukee I was approached by one of my college students who told me that as a child he had been horribly sexually abused by an Ojibwe man. He told me that this man kept child pornography, befriended his mother to gain her trust, and then convinced her to send her young son to live with him for extended periods of time, all with devastating impact. I was disgusted with the actions of his perpetrator. And my heart hurt for this guy. As I helped him figure out how to access various healing ceremonies and drove him to many myself, he named his perpetrator. It was my longtime mentor, Earl (Nyholm) Otchingwanigan.

Even though Earl had never acted inappropriately with me in any way, I believed his victim. He spoke the truth. I had kept Earl on a pedestal for many years, and now my heart was breaking. He was not who I thought he was. This young man did not want to press charges or publicly reveal his identity as a victim, and I had to honor that. But I also could not give Earl a pass. He was still in a position of power as a professor of the language and a mentor to many. I informed the FBI Child Exploitation Task Force. I informed his close contacts who had minor children. News got back to Earl quickly. Within a matter of weeks, he quit his job at Bemidji State University, emptied his office, and moved from Minnesota to Michigan.

Earl perpetrated one more crime after that. But eventually, this victim pressed charges. Evidence was gathered. He was convicted and sentenced. And he will serve the rest of his life in prison, where he needs to be. But this was still a loss, and all the uglier because it came with stinging shame for so many who believed in him and because it reflected negatively on the language community: a true language warrior was actually a criminal who hurt children. I have struggled since then about what to do with the wonderful knowledge he gave me. I settled into acceptance that this deeply flawed criminal could not be excused for his behavior, but that the language and culture he knew was itself not flawed just because one of its practitioners was. I had to carry on.

I also lost young friends. James Hardy in particular, was an unbelievable loss. He was a few years younger than me and lived just a few miles away. We attended most of the drum ceremonies together for years, hunted, traveled, and studied medicines, played chess, and visited and recorded elders together. He was on his way to becoming a ceremonial drum chief himself at Leech Lake. But he worked in the wood-treatment plant at Potlatch Lumber Mill and fell into a vat of chemicals. He got acute lymphoblastic leukemia and died a few months later.

There were other young language and culture warriors who also fell too young. Their early departures impacted not just the work but me and all the other language warriors they worked with: Sean Fahrlander, Nathan Morris, Chuck Bruce, Dan Jones, and many more. At the same time that these losses reverberated through my personal life and the broader work I was engaged in, they brought everyone left behind closer together. New language warriors were emerging and connecting with one another. I had the great privilege of walking through the losses and building community with Keller Paap, Lisa LaRonge, Dustin Burnette, Nick Hanson, Michael Sullivan, Dennis Jones, John Morrow, George Morrow, Rick and Penny Kagigebi, Persia Erdrich, Monique Paulson, Kim Anderson, Adrian Liberty, Henry Flocken, Charles Grolla, Jason Stark, Mark Pero, John Daniel, Brooke Ammann, Melissa Boyd, Chato Gonzalez, and my siblings Megan, Micah, and David Treuer.

I moved back to Bemidji in 1999, taking a new job as professor of Ojibwe at Bemidji State University. I was now closer to most of my ceremony spaces and language resources. I moved into the little cabin that had been my childhood home for many years. It was small and rustic, but still held a big place in my heart.

A lot of things were going well, but this became a time of huge personal losses and distractions too. I tell you this because our language journeys are inseparable from our personal lives, and these changes reverberated for the next decade of my life. My wife and I divorced, and I had to navigate custody and divorce courts, eventually moving all of us to northern Minnesota and guaranteeing me half-time custody of my firstborn. But that meant having her half of the time, not every day, and that impacted my language transmission plans for Giizhigookwe.

I rebounded into my next relationship, and it was a total disaster. In the span of three years, we married and had two children together—and then she descended into the darkness of drug addiction and could not emerge. The only healthy way forward was without her. Social services took her three children from her previous relationships. I loved them as my own, so I went to those hearings and advocated for the kids. In the end, I wound up with custody of both of our biological children and all three of her other children. I was now single parenting a large family, growing my professional ambitions, and maintaining an active ceremonial life. I felt truly blessed, but I was also in pain from my broken marriages and under a lot of stress. It took me years of hustle, patience, and hard lessons, but I got myself centered and healthy. I fell in love again and built a beautiful, healthy relationship. We married in 2008. I had help and support at home. And we had more children. Our family is big and blended—nine kids in all.

Not all distractions involved loss. I started publishing books and enjoyed great success with my career. My family was growing. My career was growing. My time was saturated. Everything I said yes to pushed something else off my plate. I had to really think hard about preserving as sacred a certain amount of time for my relationships, my children, my parents, my lodge, my drum commitments, my language teaching, and my language learning. Sometimes I got out of balance. Sometimes a new book or a new kid pulled time from other vital and important things. I'm an outgoing introvert. So while I wasn't shy, I needed some alone time to recharge my batteries. I adopted the "pay myself first" idea and got in some self-care at the start of each day. I had to rotate focus between personal projects and professional duties. Sometimes I took on a new book or other major project—a true time sink—and poured myself into it. But one of the beauties of projects like that is that when they are done, they are done. They could be promoted as part of everything else I did. And they amplified my voice for greater effect.

Some education professionals really seem to struggle with questions like, "How do I connect to the community?" I have never had to ask that question. I have instead asked, "How can I be the community? How can I serve my people?" I didn't have to think about how to make the lodge people happy; I worked my butt off in the lodge. I didn't have to think about how to connect with drum people; I represented and worked at the drums. I didn't worry about connecting with any political faction; we all believed in many of the same things—health, education, financial prosperity for the people, sovereignty, the environment. I cared about and worked for those things.

Indians can be really hard on each other. I remember my mom's sage advice: "Indian country is small, and someone who is giving you a hard time today will be someone you need to help you tomorrow. Be good to everyone." I adopted that disposition. The best protection was to be good to people. I did my best to stay thick-skinned and impenetrable to all the gossip and disbelief. And I treated everyone else with as much sensitivity as I could muster.

One time I was chatting in Ojibwe with Dennis Jones, when he was a newly hired Ojibwe instructor on the University of Minnesota campus and I was a graduate student there. We walked into a classroom where another professor was preparing to teach a different indigenous studies class. The professor and some of the students overheard our conversation in Ojibwe but couldn't understand it. Then the professor interrupted us, calling us "language droppers." She accused us of using the language to out-Indian other people. It was a passive-aggressive attempt to muzzle us, to shut down our use of Ojibwe to appease the professor's authority and comfort with the English language. I was hurt, but kindly defiant: "We are not language droppers. We are language users. There is a difference." And instead of being bitter and resentful toward her, I continued to show her respect and kindness over the years to come. She ended up being a good friend and supporter.

The crabs-in-a-bucket dynamic haunted me as it does any-one who tries to climb somewhere. Some people said I was too white, because I had a formal education or because I had a white father. Some said I was too backward, because I advocated for culture and language. Some said I was a profiteer, because I had career success. Some said I didn't belong in a community, because I wasn't from there. Sometimes I was hurt. Sometimes I shrugged it off. I always smiled, stepped forward, shook their hands, and did the work. And in the long run, most people appreciated me for that.

I also struggled with a balancing act. As I grew and the Ojibwe language revitalization movement grew, my email inbox and phone were blowing up every day, outrageously. If I did not answer emails about spell-checking the Ojibwe for a new slogan, program name, office plaque, or obituary notice, they wouldn't use the Ojibwe or they would get it wrong. If I just gave them names of other people to contact, they might get frustrated and give up. So a timely response really mattered. At the same time, people were happy to use me as window dressing or to validate their work. I needed to make sure that I represented the language revitalization movement and genu-inely helped, but also that I was not used or taken advantage of. I had to put my time where it would have impact.

I found practical tools really helpful too. I used an app to filter my email. I set up a website and put resources there so I didn't have to email the same things over and over. I set up automated appointments on the website so I could set avail-ability parameters and people could always find a time to catch my undivided attention.

* * *

Learning an indigenous language is a powerful decolonizing act. Our people have been through so much. They continue to suffer so much. But connecting with the language is connecting with the ancestors, the land, and authentic indigenous knowledge. It is a genuine pathway to peace and healing.

I think often of my daughter Giizhigookwe. I remember her so vividly as a one-year-old, waking in the middle of the night and crying in Ojibwe, "Baakaakonan. Indoomooday. Gegoo niwii-minikwen. (Open up. My bottle. I want something to drink)." And I remember the horrible pain we both experienced as we had each other only half of the time and my half started to fill up with other people. She had to share me with the rest of the world. But I remember too how proud I have been to watch her graduate from college, having taken four years of classes with me, signing up for the adult Ojibwe-medium program Ojibwemotaadidaa Omaa Gidakiiminaang, which means "Let's Speak Ojibwe to One Another Here on Earth," or OOG, for short, and engaging in her own language journey. She is doing transcription work in Ojibwe and is a high-level speaker. In 2019, I observed her, as part of a major language project we were both working on at Mille Lacs, take stories in dictation from James Mitchell (a great Mille Lacs first speaker), and then edit the transcriptions on an overhead projector in front of fourteen first speakers and just as many language experts, including the founders of Waadookodaading, John Nichols and others. The same year she gave the invocation at our collegiate awards banquet entirely in Ojibwe. From the little girl running around the podium saying, "Ingii-poogid," she had become the grown woman controlling the podium in Ojibwe all by herself. She is likely to raise her children in an Ojibwe language environment.

It's not easy. It's not perfect. But it is happening. Mary Roberts would be proud of us all.

My language journey is full of ups and downs. It is hard work. I loved. I lost. I loved more and more deeply. I lost more and more deeply. I found sobering humility, and I found boundless hope. There is no silver bullet, but there are lots of lessons. And I have never been alone. I have the spirits with me always, and a broad array of true friends of all ages who believe in this effort every bit as much as I do. We catch each other, inspire each other, and still plod alongside one another, crying and laughing in equal measure.

HOW WE DID IT

||||||||||||||||||||||||||||||||||||||||||||||||||

Transforming Love of the Language into a Movement

WHEN YOU FALL IN LOVE WITH YOUR CHILD, THE FIRST THING you ask yourself is, "What does my baby need?" And then you fill the need. The health of your beloved child depends on your doing so. When you fall in love with your language, its health similarly depends on you. So first ask yourself not what you need, certainly not what your tribal chairman or boss or neighbor needs, but instead, "What does my language need?"

The answer to that question will point the way. Depending on the demographics of your language community, the resources already developed, the number and location of your living speakers, and the motivation and commitment of others who value the language, your language will need things that are different from what someone else's needs. And it may have different needs now than it did a decade ago. What does your language need?

We were able to identify numerous critical needs for Ojibwe. We need speakers. There are a quarter of a million Ojibwe people in the United States and Canada, but only forty thousand speakers at best. Most are elders. We need the speakers to teach. We need people to learn—specifically, we need *young* people to learn. We need schools and programs to change credentialing so we can put the speakers in teaching positions. We need teacher-training programs. We need books: one-word-per-page books, young-reader books, Harry Potter books in Ojibwe. We need our own indigenous literature in our own language. And we need many thousands of books, not five. We need them now. We need curricula. We need tribal-language-medium schools. We need day-care facilities that are language nests. We need information and data. We don't even have a good head count of how many speakers we have. We need more dictionaries. And not just ones that translate from Ojibwe to English but ones in Ojibwe with Ojibwe definitions of the words, without English. We need money. We need grants. We need endowments. We need leadership and more leadership. We need people to step up and provide initiative and expertise. We need tribal support. We need road signs in Ojibwe. We need help justifying our existence to the rest of the world. We need help convincing our own people why the language matters. We need a respite from all the deaths and overdoses and poverty, from corporate and governmental parasites and missionaries clawing at our timber, our minerals, our water, our workers, and our souls. We need social services to serve and support, not break up, our families. We need permission to write our own rule books for educational standards and testing and assessment. We need healthy ceremonies. We need time to nourish our own spiritual development. We need to really exhaustively identify all our needs.

We also need a break from being the ones who try to meet all the needs, but that isn't going to happen. Carl Jung once said, "Who looks outside dreams; who looks inside awakes."[4] Don't look around the corner; look in the mirror. Margaret Mead once said, "Never doubt that a small group of thoughtful committed citizens can change the world; indeed, it's the only thing that ever has."[5] Who are those thoughtful, committed citizens? You are. You are the one you've been waiting for. Nobody is going to do it for you.

And so—what do you need?

Darrell Kipp, founder of the Piegan Institute, said there is only one attitude necessary to get you started on language revitalization: "Do not ask for permission. Don't beg. Don't debate."[6] Don't fight. Just do the work. You will get slammed by white, brown, and black folks who don't see the value of what you are doing. You will get it from your own people. Professional educators will be in your way. So will government officials and social workers and health care professionals. Sometimes they will resist you and the rest of the time they will ignore you. They will be too busy or self-absorbed to answer your emails. Some may appreciate you, but few will help. There is a mountain of inertia. Be the movement. Be the change. No apologies. Anyone in the way just wants to suck the energy and joy out of your sacred mission. Smile, shake their hands. Then step right past them and speak to your baby. Open your computer. Grab your phone. Go to the school. Go to the ceremony. Do the work.

Do the work even if you are the only one doing the work. You can't wait. Do treasure any partners who join you. Do accept help. Do find the money. But don't wait for any of those things. You can't convince everyone. And you don't need to. Take a triage approach. If someone needs convincing, they will take too much of your precious time. Send them a YouTube link to an inspiring language video or send them a book. Then get back to work.

You can't save your language in all urban, Native communities, on all reservations, or in every community fairly and equally all the time. You simply have to save the language.

Then you can grow the connection points and opportunities and proliferate the effort.

Reforming broken systems of oppression will not work. We have to build new systems of liberation. Public schools are a white-empowerment program. They only ever achieve that end result—the empowerment of white students. But not our students. Not our sacred babies. Not our way or in our ways. Those schools will take our babies and empower them to be white, but never empower them to be who they are. Those of us who survived such systems survived in spite of what the institutions did to us, rather than because of what they did for us. We need an indigenous-empowerment program. The language is the key to making that possible. We need to build it. No one else can. No one else will. Our bank of speakers is not likely to grow if we wait. Time is of the essence.

Our languages have been under systematic assault for many generations. Their salvation will require a systematic response. Our approach to this work has to be both ancient and modern. Indigenize your toolbox and organize for change.

Be smart about the governance and structure of any organization you build. Failure to be attentive to these details means that you will build your big, beautiful, critically important language house on a foundation of sand instead of stone. You will make everything you do unnecessarily vulnerable. Whole schools and language programs have been gutted because of weak governance and unarticulated goals. Even though founding documents and paperwork and mission statements might seem nonindigenous, a foundation of feelings with no structure can shift as fast as the emotions of even one team member. These things are only nonindigenous if we don't indigenize them.

Plan smart. Use an adaptive leadership approach. The demography of your language community will change quickly. The economic, political, and social issues your people face every day are always shifting. You will lose speakers as elders pass. You will gain new speakers as programs and schools mature and grow. What you build has to be able to adapt to these rapidly changing dynamics that influence all the people you want to engage with your effort.

Keep it simple. You can get really bogged down trying to please everyone and represent every constituency in your community. That can set you up for conflict. I recommend *not* vesting the control of a school or program in the tribe itself. The election cycles will come every couple of years, and that means the pet projects and support will swing like a pendulum. It's stronger to have a separate, 501(c)(3) nonprofit organization to control your money and employ your team. If you go that route, use the minimum-size board for your nonprofit. Right now, that means a three-person board. You can establish working groups and committees for whatever parts of the work require more direct engagement. This will streamline your decision-making process and reduce the risk of politicizing the emerging work.

White organizational structure and governance—*Robert's Rules of Order* and democratic processes where someone always loses a political argument and ideas compete with one another for attention and action—are for white organizations. Don't use a control-and-competition culture to impose anything on Indigenous people, who thrive best with a cooperative approach to problem-solving. If you use a more cooperative governance structure, you will avoid more problems, which will enable you to focus on the language work.

Most tribes have a highly colonized operating culture that is riddled with oppression dynamics. Be careful. You don't want your sacred mission to be dismantled by a couple of cranky people or wither on the vine because someone forces a new agenda on you after you get started.

Here is a cautionary tale and true story. The Leech Lake Reservation in northern Minnesota has a Bureau of Indian Education school called the Bug-O-Nay-Ge-Shig School. It's named after one of our famous local chiefs. Leech Lake is in the heart of Ojibwe country. In the early 2000s, plenty of people there, young and old, wanted to begin working on language. Discussion was underway about making a tribal-language-medium program—a school within the Bug-O-Nay-Ge-Shig School—to teach all day long exclusively in Ojibwe.

I was present for some of the early discussions, including when John Mitchell suggested the name *Niigaane* (He Leads) for the program. It was really exciting. The Leech Lake tribe's school board is elected by tribal membership and answers directly to the tribal council. I recommended taking the extra time to build a nonprofit or charter operation so as to avoid tribal control, but I was working at the university in Bemidji and wouldn't be on the ground when the program started. My voice didn't have much traction on that point, and understandably everyone just wanted to get started.

The initial success of the program was staggering. The teachers and families were really dedicated to the effort. The kids were getting the language. The community was getting engaged and energized by the effort. But eventually the tribe started to cut funding, then restored funding, then cut it again. It was disruptive to the delivery of the program. Grant dollars, too, came in spurts.

There are never enough teachers who are fluent in Ojibwe. Niigaane and other Ojibwe-medium programs had to build their own. So they paired fluent elders with advanced, second-language learners and ran the classes in Ojibwe. It worked.

The teachers usually had credentials and significant target-language ability, and the elders in the classrooms enabled the teachers to grow at the same time that together they immersed the kids.

Then came the real test. Stretching to cover the growing size of the program, Niigaane hired a new, second-language learner as one of the teachers, as they had done many times before. But the new teacher did not believe in Ojibwe-medium education, thinking instead that immersing the kids would stunt their English-language development and other core academic aptitudes. The teacher turned to the new superintendent, challenging the idea of Ojibwe immersion. His actions showed that he did not believe in the mission of the school, but since this challenge came from inside the program, the new superintendent listened. Test scores in English and math were her top priority, and she couldn't see the value of teaching in Ojibwe. The superintendent fired some of the key staff—head teachers who had anchored the program for years. Others quit in protest.

Who was left standing, after all the drama? The superintendent and the guy who challenged the mission. Then two elder speakers, who instead of training the staff in language and talking to the kids every day, all day, had to provide Ojibwe enrichment in an English-language classroom environment. Some of the families quit the program. Others stayed. Nobody's test scores improved. But the program was no longer an immersion program, and the kids no longer spoke Ojibwe to one another on the playground. It was a travesty. It was also preventable, had they done more work up front to build a structure that was more resistant to tribal politics or a rogue staff member. Just this year, the program hired a great language speaker as head classroom teacher, and he's working hard to reestablish Ojibwe-medium discipline in the classroom, but it is a long road and there is still resistance. There is cause for hope at Niigaane in spite of the damage and major setback.

Have you ever sat through one of those mission-statement exercises and just wished they would pull something off the internet and leave you alone? I usually feel like that, especially if it's in a big organization. By the time everyone weighs in and wordsmiths the statement, with all the little contributions included so someone can impress their coworker or boss, it boils down to "we believe in education." As I said, they could have just pulled it off the internet and not wasted my time. But have you ever been part of an exercise like that where all your stakeholders were engaged and your thinking about your core values, goals, and mission was crystallized? I actually have seen that happen too, and it can be truly transformative.

The Native Hawaiian language movement stands out in my mind as a perfect example of this. At its lowest point, there were only one thousand speakers of Hawaiian left on Earth. Half lived in the isolated island community of Ni'ihau, and the other five hundred were elders scattered across all the other islands. Just thirty years ago, it was illegal to use the language in public schools. Today it is one of Hawaii's official state languages, and there are around twenty-two thousand speakers of Hawaiian. There are twenty-two Hawaiian-medium schools operating across the state, and a student can go from kindergarten through high school, and even to college, in a Hawaiian-medium educational environment. This did not happen by accident. It was and remains a huge job—lots of work, dedication, and effort. But it was made possible through a calculated, organizational effort that began with a soul-searching and inclusive effort to identify core Hawaiian cultural values: aloha (love, kindness), ohana (family), kuleana (responsibility), laulima (cooperation), kokua (help), ike (recognition), ho'oponopono (forgiveness), kupono (honesty), and lokahi (peace, unity, harmony). These often resonate with people from many cultures, but they are foundational in their true Hawaiian context. The educational planners were committed to squaring everything they did with those values, and their application in Hawaiian-medium schools is powerful.

At the start of each school day, the entire staff (teachers, cooks, janitors, and administrators) lines up in rows in front of the school. The kids get dropped off—in buses, in cars, by straggling parents—but they don't go in the school; they line up in rows facing the staff. Then the kids initiate contact and communication through song. When the staff feels that kids are sincere, they sing back and welcome the children to school. Then every kid gets a hug from everyone who works there every day. Aloha!

I can hear white administrators in mainstream schools viewing this with incredulity. What? They want to spend forty-five minutes on cultural enrichment *every day*? The kids are awake then. They should do math. Have you seen our math scores? But consider that at most schools, truancy rates for Indigenous kids and students of color are much higher than the rates for white kids. The truancy rate in Red Lake Middle School is typically around 50 percent every day. *Half the kids are not there.* Six full classes of kids enter kindergarten every year, but by their senior year of high school there are not enough kids to fill one classroom.

The Hawaiian-medium schools have very low truancy rates. Outsiders see the cultural enrichment activities as cultural enrichment only, but to Hawaiians they are core indigenous values being centered in the lives of their children, and the centering of Hawaiian beliefs gets the kids engaged in the school and everything the staff is trying to teach them. If someone wants to get from New York to Seattle, they could start running now, or they could get a bus, load up the kids, and step on the gas. Who's going to get there first, with the most kids? Speaking to someone in a way that respects their core cultural values gets them on the bus. Aloha is the Hawaiian way.

When a child enrolls in a Hawaiian-medium school, it is not only the child who matriculates but the entire family. Each family has to pick flowers and leaves from plants whose names have double meanings that signify important characteristics: koa for bravery, kukui for enlightenment, and others. Then they weave a lei piko—a giant lei that goes over the door to the school. Piko means umbilical cord, and the lei symbolizes the connection to previous generations. Ohana.

When there are discipline issues at the Hawaiian-medium schools, they do not assign punishment to individuals. They rehabilitate relationships between people. Lokahi. If Joey hits Johnny, they assemble the whole school under the lei their families wove and Joey has to lomi, or work the bad stuff out. And after that, he gets a hug from everyone in the school. Ho'oponopono.

While what the Hawaiians do might seem novel or neat to non-Hawaiians, it is the key to their self-stated goal: to make healthy humans with strong mauli (spiritual fire). The children don't just attend these schools to learn their language and culture. They use their language and culture, obtained from the schools, home, and community, to excel academically and socially as Hawaiians and citizens of the world. The data from these schools shows that their methods produce the academic excellence, high graduation rates, and upward mobility we want all kids of all backgrounds to achieve. The clearly defined, value-driven approach is truly effective. When you are ready to get real about your language, you need to identify your cultural values and organize everything you do around them.

I had been well aware of the exciting developments around Hawaiian-medium education for years, but starting in 2010, I got a close-up, personal look. Patrick Welle, a white colleague of mine at Bemidji State University, asked me to help him coordinate our university's Hawaiian Field Program. It previously had a focus on environmental studies. With Welle's blessing, we began to transform the program into an indigenous field program. It's now housed formally in BSU's Ojibwe Program, as an indigenous languages field program. Through a number of trips to the Big Island and sustained interaction with staff at the University of Hawaii–Hilo and Ke Kula 'O Nwahokalani'pu'u Iki Lab Public Charter School (Nwah), I was able to bring groups of undergraduate students, usually twenty at a time, to the best Hawaiian programs in the world. Experiential learning is powerful in any circumstance, but with the Hawaiians, it was truly moving.

Even if we got to the Big Island in January, when school was not in session, staff members insisted on coming in from their holidays to meet us at the school. They always got there first, lined up, and waited for us to enter the school in the Hawaiian custom. That meant I had to line up twenty Minnesotans in straight rows and make them initiate communication by singing to the assembled Hawaiians. The discomfort was always palpable. I usually helped them sing and prepared them to speak. But when they were done and Hawaiians sang back and then proceeded to hug everyone in my class and welcome them to the school, many of my students were usually crying. After all, they were from Minnesota, where singing and hugging are not your usual academic activities. We didn't just watch videos and tour the facilities. We learned about hula and history. We saw how the kids there farmed taro plants at the schools and produced a lot of their own food. We saw educational principles and language revitalization in action.

But we cannot do what the Hawaiians do in a non-Hawaiian context. We have to explore what that would look like in each of our respective contexts. That means introspection and authentic cultural knowledge.

In an Ojibwe context, many people hold up values defined in a variation of the Seven Grandfather Teachings: debwewin (truth), mino-dabasenindizowin (humility), manaajitwaawin (respect), zhawendaagoziwin (love), gwayakowaadiziwin (honesty), zoongide'ewin (courage), and nibwaakaawin (wisdom). There have been a number of schools, programs, and language initiatives that have tried to establish these as the context for their work. It is an emerging effort in our part of the world, but one that holds great promise.

When we do things our way, our people are inspired. When Niigaane first got started, the team was hunting for more fluent first speakers of Ojibwe to pull into the program. As the children started running around the cafeteria, speaking Ojibwe to one another, an unlikely candidate emerged. His name was Mark Wakanabo. He was unlikely only because he was shy and quiet by nature. His language skills were quite fantastic. He was also already employed by the Bug-O-Nay-Ge-Shig School, which housed Niigaane, as a janitor for many years. He stepped up, saying, "Indoojibwem (I speak Ojibwe)." He dropped his broom and never picked it up again. He ran with the kids every day. After several years of working in the program, he suffered a heart attack and was rushed to the hospital and defibrillated. He was back at work the next day, in violation of doctor's orders, wanting to work. His chest was still puffy from the defibrillation. But he was so inspired by the kids and the mission that he wanted to be there. The other staff were a little freaked out and eventually convinced him to go home and rest, but it was still a powerful testament to the engaging power of indigenous language. When you speak someone's language, they get you. And the passion is contagious.

Once you have defined your cultural values and articulated them in the value and mission statements for your program or school, then it is critical to square your institutional and individual actions with these values. If someone is straying from the mission, wasting time on a pet project, getting distracted by the politics, or tearing down others, tell them, "We all hold one another accountable to these values. How does this teach our kids respect, love, honesty, and wisdom?"

*   *   *

When developing the value statements, mission statements, and goals, it is also important to be wary of pitfalls that are deeply ingrained in our communities and our people, even our most culturally minded people. It can be very hard to see ourselves. We have all been deeply impacted by the colonial experience. As a result, we all house many attributes of dominant culture inside of us. We may think about money, operate materialistically, or value the pursuit of money over other critical objectives without even noticing we are doing so. We may judge or ostracize members of our own community, thinking we have good reasons, but not realizing that our "good reasons" just gave us permission to countermand a value of cooperation or consensus. As previously mentioned, Paulo Freire defines these as oppression dynamics. Our internalized oppression (shame and self-blame), lateral oppression (crab-in-the-bucket thinking; meanness to our own people), intra-oppressed group oppression (racism, sexism, homophobia), and external oppression (racism from outside) all support English dominance and white supremacy, even though only one of those pillars comes from outside of our communities.

Embracing our languages and cultures is not primitive. It will not slow down our kids. It will teach them the most valuable skills for their success in the world. But some of our own people won't believe that. When you get started, it is critical to be aware of how insidious such beliefs are, so they don't permeate the work space or founding principles in any way.

At the same time, many of our traditional-minded people may be skeptical of *any* formal educational institution. Their reasons are perfectly understandable, considering everything our people have been through with residential boarding schools and other assimilation policies. But we have always educated our young. The problem isn't education. It's educational institutions and educators operating with a colonial mind-set, within a colonial operating culture, and using a colonial language. If we decolonize the educational process and institutions that carry on the process, then education can be as it was in the beginning for us—liberating.

Another area of caution in launching a major movement is around the practice of dependency. Our people were independent, self-reliant, and highly capable for many thousands of years prior to the colonization era. But the treaty period eroded our self-reliance. The US government orchestrated the annihilation of sixty million buffalo, while troops sent to subdue us destroyed our crops and orchards. Many tribes—undefeated in battle but unable to survive—surrendered, signing treaties that traded land for promises of food, education, and tools for making a life without our land base. Once the tribes surrendered, lumber and hydro companies ruined wild rice beds, and farmers raising cash crops plowed the prairies under and drained the life-giving marshes. The government issued rations. Instead of producing our own food, we increasingly depended on a non-tribal entity to provide many of our basic needs. We got rations of lard and flour and made fry bread. Our health declined. Our resources and even knowledge of self-sufficiency declined. Food control is people control. The more the government controlled our food, the more we were controlled. And there were few good choices. We have to reassert control of our food and everything else. We have to be more self-reliant.

Food control was only one way to manufacture tribal dependence on the US government. Dependency can take many forms. Parents make rules for their kids and control their agendas. The government twisted our diplomats' customary uses of familial terms, which invoked healthy family relationships, into language that asserted paternalistic control, like "great white father" for the president and "little red children" for tribes. The apparatuses of dependency are still fully deployed. The US government still holds tribal lands in trust and manages them as the custodian or guardian of tribal people. The government routinely mismanaged income from those lands and finally settled an enormous class-action lawsuit, *Cobell v. Salazar*, for $3.4 billion in 2009. This lawsuit is just one more chapter in a very long book of paternalism gone wrong.

After 1934, when the US government passed the Indian Reorganization Act, the white Indian agents who were running reservations started to be replaced by tribal leaders in many functions of tribal governance, enabling tribes to assert more self-determination. The political culture on reservations was in a state of great disrepair, to say the least. Tribal people expected someone to take care of them. As a result, tribal citizens began to look to their tribal governments with a sense of imposed obligation—the tribal government is there to provide them with financial resources, jobs, housing, and propane. This is still the feeling today. And many tribes now have a greater degree of economic independence. Any tribal leader who doesn't make it rain has a short political life expectancy. So tribal leaders get grant writers to bring in money to create jobs, begging for the scraps from Uncle Sam's table. I am not saying they should not write grants. I am saying that being in a state of permanently begging and expecting diminishes the self-reliance more intrinsic to our cultures.

As a result of these historical and contemporary practices, tribal people are often acclimated to dependency. When we want to get something going, we look to our tribal, state, provincial, or federal governments to provide the impetus, the money, the skilled people, and the buildings, and to pay for the heat and make it happen. We expect this. And when our expectations are not met, we get discouraged and give up, retreating to our private domains with a sense of bitter resignation and complaining instead of stepping up and being the change agents ourselves. The reasons for this attitude are understandable. We gave up an entire continent for a handful of empty promises. But understandable though that attitude is, it is simply ineffective, and a certain death for tribal languages. We have to change.

We are the change. We are the leaders. We have to make our own luck. We have to be grateful to our resilient ancestors and elders who maintained our cultures through terrible times, and we must very intentionally nurture and pass these gifts down to our future generations. The world is not a fair place. We have to make our own fairness. It should not be that way, but it is. We have to navigate an imposed cultural climate of dependency with compassion for our people and some fire-in-the-belly, nothing-can-stop-me, I-will-make-my-own-luck leadership.

Otherwise the great work on values and mission and goals will die on the spot. Included in those cultural values should be hard work, self-determination, and manifest sovereignty.

* * *

An emerging language revitalization effort has to be adaptive to succeed. While there should be unwavering commitment to shared values and goals, the tools to meet those goals must be able to adapt to rapidly changing dynamics in our communities. When we started our work with Ojibwe, there were many thousands of first speakers, and every Ojibwe community had some. But there were very few successful second-language learners of Ojibwe. Now, a few decades later, there are many fewer first speakers—and many more second-language learners.

New problems have emerged. How do we keep challenging and elevating the aptitude of advanced, second-language learners? We didn't have that problem when we first started. How do we develop succession plans as our great first speakers pass away—succession plans in ceremonial circles, educational circles, and everywhere else those elders are needed? We have to be able to adapt. Similarly, as new technologies emerge, there are new blessings and barriers—tools to advance the work, but also distractions and financial pressure to get the latest for our schools. For Ojibwe, some dialects have dominated in the publication of dictionaries and story anthologies in the language. How do we use these resources to teach in places where the dialects are different and less well supported? Everyone has something to learn. Everyone has something to teach.

Because language revitalization is not a super-seasoned, multi-decade effort with more people doing the work than there is work to do, another of its weaknesses is that our language warriors are stretched very thin. We burn out our first-speaker leaders. Big, critical pieces of the work are under-addressed or dropped altogether. Leaders get used as window dressing by those who want to show off culture rather than live it. The best way to interrupt these tendencies is to have high expectations for *everyone* who gets engaged *at any level*. We must hold one another to account—we must be true to our values, work hard, and give at full capacity based on our respective strengths. That will naturally weed out folks just trying to look good. It will allow the work to be shared more fairly with less burnout. When someone tries to pressure or criticize, it will cause them to back off if they, in turn, are asked to step up.

When humans believe that they are experiencing great abundance, they naturally and more commonly act on their better impulses and align their actions with the stated values of their people, religions, and governments. But when people believe they are experiencing serious scarcity, they are more likely to abandon the ideals of kindness, charity, cooperation, and sharing, and are more likely to be adversarial, defensive, or reactive. Native people have experienced and continue to experience genuine scarcity in many areas of their lives, and their perception of scarcity is even higher. I noticed that even for my mother, who experienced brutal poverty as a child, scarcity was a disposition that persisted even after she found financial success as an attorney. We always joked that we could take that woman off the rez, but we could never take the rez out of that woman. In a very real sense, as you get going on language revitalization, scarcity response and defensiveness will create barriers for you, inside your communities and out.

In *The Anatomy of Peace*, Duane Boyce lays out a really impressive method for generating influence with other people, even if those people won't talk to you. It's both introspective and outer-directed. Working on your grounding and authenticity

is the starting point. Fully humanizing the people you inter-
act with is at the heart of the effort. He describes how to work
on relationships and generate influence with people, who can
then influence others. His method is sound and really useful in
many contexts, including community development and building relationships for language revitalization.

Most of the thirty Mayan languages had writing systems
before contact. Other indigenous languages developed writing
systems and even literary traditions early in the contact period.
Such was the case for Hawaiian. There were numerous newspapers published in Hawaiian that were widely read by the
Hawaiian-speaking population; these are still available. But for
most other tribal languages, it was missionaries who came in
the 1600s, 1700s, or 1800s who developed the first writing systems for those languages. Some people challenge the need for
a writing system or writing of any kind at all. They say, "That's
not our way. That's not traditional." I am usually thinking, "You
drove here in a car to tell me it's not traditional to write our
language?" But I say that we are in a different time. I say that
writing a book can enable someone to bring the language with
them wherever they go. It can preserve words, phrases, and stories for generations to come. Our languages are under assault,
and we need all the tools we can find to engineer their protection and growth.

For tribes that spanned a large geographic area, like the
Lakota, Blackfeet, or Ojibwe, different missionaries worked
simultaneously in different places and came up with radically
different writing systems for the same languages. Ojibwe has
three active writing systems: folk phonetics, syllabics, and double vowel. The confusion about writing the language, and with
which system, is compounded by other dynamics in a language
community. Most tribal-language speakers in the United States

and Canada and throughout the British Commonwealth are bilingual. They speak English and their tribal language. They learned English in school, which means they first learned how to write in English. For them, it is easiest to use their deeply ingrained knowledge of how to write in English to write words as they sound. This is called folk phonetics, and it makes perfect sense to bilinguals whose first language is a tribal language. The problem with folk phonetics is that three speakers may end up writing a word three different ways, and what is obvious to any one of those speakers is not obvious to other speakers or students of the language. Who wants to tell their beloved, sometimes cranky, deeply knowledgeable first speakers that their way of writing isn't working?

The result is an all-too-common war of writing systems, which can be off-putting, discouraging, or even fatal for an emerging language revitalization movement. Don't go there. We had some growing pains in the Ojibwe language revitalization universe due to this. But we are increasingly in front of it now. The writing system (or systems) has to be consistent to have the greatest ease of use for students. Our fluent speakers were most interested in hearing their grandkids speak the language. Once they could see that happening, they started to get on board. We didn't argue with anybody. That's a lateral-oppression trap. We just did the work. We wrote the books; we published the dictionaries. We worked on lexical expansion of the language to cover new technologies and mathematical concepts. We developed literature. We worked with every kind of press willing to publish our work. We developed a real market for this material, and publishers started to pay serious attention. And as we gained more momentum, our elders saw the merits. Some of the most stalwart resisters to a standardized writing system were converted and now actively publish in double vowel, which has been the standard for most new publications in Ojibwe. The old stuff in other writing systems is still of great use for reference, but—without a fight—we have charted a course and kept our great first speakers on the bus and even in the driver's seat, strengthening the writing system and the corpus of work all along the way.

For many tribal languages, dialect wars can be just as disruptive as writing system wars—and sometimes even more so. The variations in dialect are sometimes very significant. But they are often less important than some would have you believe. It's important to know what is gained and what is lost by how much you limit yourself to one particular dialect or how much you expand into others. Many languages are simply past the point of even being able to be picky. But here too, we discovered a liberating way to do the work without losing any stakeholders or chasing anyone away from the language effort. We decided that all dialects are correct; we don't have to pick only one for a book or a school. We can document many at the same time and use many at the same time. We sometimes worked simultaneously with nine different dialects. When speakers diverged on how a word was spoken in two different places, we put both words in the dictionary and noted which dialect each was from. That got rid of the fighting and fear and got people cooperating on the work with great results.

Beware of other divisions that can alienate our people and supporters. There should be no race wars. No pedigree fights. No attempts to out-Indian one another. We need everyone. We should appreciate everyone who is leaning into this effort and put them to work. We should not fight our own warriors. We must save the language. Full stop.

*   *   *

With clear values, missions, and goals, and with a full awareness of the pitfalls and problems out there, the next most
important decision is to settle on the best method to win this
war. Then stick to the plan and feed it daily with overwhelming effort. There are many methods, and all have merit. Here is
what I have seen work.

Use your target language as the medium for everything.
Every successful language revitalization effort does this one way
or another. Whether it is a tribal-language-medium school or a
master-apprentice model, the target language—the language
you most want to live—needs to become the language you use
to talk about the language, to make plans about the language,
to organize your institutions for the language, and especially
to become the day-to-day operating medium for delivering the
language to the people you want to learn it.

You have to be and stay strong. Use your language to deliver
the goods. It is really hard, especially when you are starting,
and it takes discipline. Maintain that discipline. Your fluent
speakers will get tired. They will want to lapse into English,
maybe just long enough to yell at the kids that recess is over.
But this is where you need your language the most. You will
have legions of doubters about this idea. You also will have
many outright resisters. They may say things like, "We want to
make sure our kids and grandkids have good English skills so
they can succeed." But hidden in statements like that are many
ideas that are simply wrong. One is that an English-language-
world's definition of success is the only kind of success that
matters or is the most important kind of success. And learning a tribal language does not cut off learning English. That
view is simply wrong. No tribal-language-medium school has
ever produced a monolingual, tribal-language speaker. Frankly,
I think that would be awesome, but they haven't done it. The

good schools produce tribal-language speakers who all speak, read, and write English just fine, and usually better than their monolingual, English-speaking peers. Stick to your guns. Make the means to get to the end you desire: fluency in your language for your people.

There is no half measure. Don't do target-language enrichment. That just means doing everything in English with a little vocabulary list and a feather to pass around during circle time. The result is kids who know ten words in their heritage language and why the feather is sacred—and nobody is speaking the tribal language.

Do not do bilingual programming. Everyone knows English too well. It's like pouring dye into a pitcher of water. You just can't get it out. Your language should have equal status with English, and the same utility. There is nothing that is done in English that we cannot do in any living tribal language. If you don't make the rules—in your language—you will be ruled—in English.

People follow the paths of least resistance, and English offers the least resistance. People with degrees speak English well, and the more degrees people have, the better their English. They did their learning in English. Even Indigenous people with degrees are programmed to have greater faith in their modern learning than in their ancestors. I am an Indigenous person with a lot of degrees. I was programmed, so I know this for a fact. As a result, we have to resist this programming. That means swimming upstream against the current of English language comfort and dominance. We need to swim hard, or our effort will drown.

The Maori and Hawaiians started their revitalization effort with a target-language nest. It began with day-care and early childhood programs. They disciplined themselves strictly for target-language use. They took the long view. They knew that to rebuild a population of speakers would take decades. The house that would shelter and instruct everyone had to have the strongest possible foundation. If their best speakers spent time only with the oldest and most advanced kids, nobody would get that foundation. So they strengthened the foundation, putting the best speakers with the youngest kids. Then, as the babies moved from day-care to early childhood programs to kindergarten, they built the next layer. One year at a time, they included a new grade in the system, until they had built out to elementary school, middle school, and high school. They didn't stop there, either. In Hawaii, they built Hawaiian-medium, teacher-training programs at colleges and universities. And now many graduates from their flagship schools have been certified as teachers and are returning to the education effort to sustain and expand the programs. The Hawaiians have twenty-two Hawaiian-medium schools, geoproximate to most of the Native Hawaiian population. The Maori have had similar success in developing the marae—sacred communal gathering places—into language nests and proliferating and scaling up their language in formal education and political environments.

You need the nests—places where people can go to use the language with no English infiltration. These can be day care, schools, language tables (done right!), immersion lunches, and master-apprentice spaces. Once these are established, you can grow the size of the nests and expand to different locations and through different venues, including some amazing possibilities with new technologies.

Stay disciplined. Use your target language as the language to do your planning. Use it as the language to build your language infrastructure and even your physical buildings. Take the time and use the tools to teach your elders how to use their language to orchestrate an immersion-teaching environment. Teach certified teachers how to orchestrate an immersion-teaching environment. The Center for Advanced Research on Language Acquisition (CARLA) at the University of Minnesota, the Indigenous Language Institute (ILI) in New Mexico, and other organizations can be helpful with trainings in immersion pedagogy, skills, and practical experience. In the classroom, use Total Physical Response (TPR) methods—body language and context clues to convey meaning—along with properly modeled language use, rather than providing translations. In no time, students will have connected the language and the meaning and be functioning in the language.

Your discipline will yield the greatest results. Remember that a child hears a language for a full year before saying his or her first word. You need to engineer an entire year's worth of listening time to start that process. If you don't use the target language exclusively, then you force that process to take much longer. Even if you had 50 percent airtime in your language, it would take twice as long to develop the ear of your students, and that assumes that hearing English could be limited to only 50 percent of the time. Stay patient with your kids and persistent with your efforts and discipline.

As your reputation grows, you will get a lot of visitors. Accommodate guests, accept their support, appreciate their interest, and court their money. But don't waver on your target-language discipline. Visitors will try to speak English in the hallways or to one another. Make literature, post signs, put it on your website, and provide an orientation to all visitors: no English allowed. If they only know English, then do not allow talking in your target-language space. This is respect.

If you are not in the vanguard launching a new school, program, or movement, then you need to take a careful inventory of what is actually happening in already established efforts. Remember that *immersion* is a buzzword in the language revitalization arena and grant-writing world. Therefore, not every so-called immersion program is truly immersive. A program doesn't do target-language-medium work just because it's framed as or called an immersion program. Look closely, and then use your influence to help shape the future direction of existing efforts.

You need data. You can waste years trying to develop data if you tell yourself you need it to start. You don't need data to start, but you do need it to grow, expand, and deepen the work. You need to know how many speakers you have; what ages they are; what your tribal population is and how much of it lives on the reservation and off the reservation, respectively; what the birth rate is; and what the surveys say about language as a priority for your people, broken down by age group. Knowing these things helps with political advocacy and grant writing, and helps you have your finger on the pulse of your community's needs.

* * *

Our governance systems, languages and cultures, economies, and bodies have been under assault systemically for generations. We face both internal and external threats. We have lost a lot, but we have retained a lot too. Rebuilding and revitalizing require a systemic response. We can't just send a few warriors over the hill and expect them to vanquish all political, economic, cultural, and linguistic threats. We have to very conscientiously build up our people as individuals and as communities.

Your language warriors need a nurturing language community, and you have to build that. Wishing it well is not enough.

I believe that most people of most heritages around the globe wish they spoke their heritage languages; but the number willing to go after those languages with everything they have is small. Build the community. Nurture one another. Protect one another. Give one another respite and relief. Use that community to share in the raising of children in protected environments—physically protected, but culturally protected and supported too.

In the Ojibwe world we have had, since time immemorial, a distinct cultural dynamic that both blesses and plagues our current efforts. There has always been a strong belief in individual spiritual empowerment. If one person dreams that they are to use certain colors for representing the four directions and to locate the door to the sweat lodge facing east, that's what they do. But if their neighbor dreams of different colors and a different direction for the door, that's what they do. This has always created great variation in cultural practices across the Ojibwe world, which often confuses outsiders. But for the Ojibwe, it's easily understood: "That's what they do there; this is what we do here." As a result of this cultural fabric, the Ojibwe have tended to be very tolerant of cultural differences within their world, but extremely intolerant of being told what to do. Even someone who gained too much influence could be shunned, pushed out, or simply abandoned. Freedom was real and really valued. So if someone was too bossy or even just too influential, someone else left them behind and moved down the river to start a new village.

This dynamic is still part of the cultural fabric, but it is exacerbated by internalized- and lateral-oppression dynamics. Leading in Ojibwe country is difficult. Starting a language revitalization effort is a leadership activity of the highest import and impact. You will meet resistance. You will need backup. It won't materialize because you deserve it or have a good idea. It must be built.

I have personally been so blessed with the company and support of great mentors. But I had to drive thousands of miles, over decades, to cultivate those relationships. And as the Ojibwe language revitalization efforts started to take real shape, there were many others who were on parallel paths. We found each other. That's when things really started to happen.

In the early 1990s, while Archie was still alive and I had started to pour myself into Ojibwe language and culture learning, my journey into Ojibwe spaces had me bumping into many young people with similar dreams. In 1992, I met the twin brothers Dan and Dennis Jones. They are from Nigigoonsiminikaaning First Nation in the Treaty Three area of northwest Ontario. They are outrageously funny. They were young then. None of us had gray hair yet. Both came to the Bemidji State University American Indian Awards Banquet. We sat together and started speaking Ojibwe. I soon began visiting their first nation on frequent fishing and hunting trips. Their mother, Nancy Jones, was and remains one of the greatest speakers of Ojibwe I have ever met. We were just having fun then. But we all were also working at universities, leaning into language work, traveling to conferences, and building networks. As the Jones brothers pulled me into language camps and projects they were working on, I pulled them into publishing in the *Oshkaabewis Native Journal* and into conferences and workshops I was engaged with. These things fed each other reciprocally, and the productivity of our individual efforts and careers increased while the friendships deepened.

As a graduate student representative at the University of Minnesota back in 1994, I was on the hiring committee for a new Ojibwe professor. We brought in Dennis Jones as the new instructor of Ojibwe. Within a few more years, the university added John Nichols, an established linguist working with Ojibwe, and the linguistics program as well as the Ojibwe language undergraduate program really started to flourish. Dan Jones moved to Cloquet and provided a major impetus for program development at Fond du Lac Tribal and Community College and throughout the Fond du Lac Reservation and greater Duluth area.

I met Keller Paap, another eager language apostle, while he was an undergraduate student at the University of Minnesota. His intellectual, spiritual, and musical gifts made him a genuine force in the Ojibwe world. Keller and his wife, Lisa LaRonge, began to dream about a bona fide tribal-language-medium school in Ojibwe country. In 2001, Keller and Lisa launched the Waadookodaading Ojibwe Language Institute in Hayward, Wisconsin. It was later moved from a charter in the public school there to a charter in the tribal school in Reserve, Wisconsin, on the reservation at Lac Courte Oreilles. It is now the oldest and most well-established Ojibwe-medium school in the world. There is more below on what they do and how they do it. Keller and Lisa both humbly stuck to the work and carefully built and expanded a team of people to take on different parts of the effort—Brooke Ammann as director, Dustin Burnette as a classroom teacher, and many more. I came to Waadookodaading often to perform evaluations of staff in Ojibwe literacy and fluency, immersion-teaching techniques, and classroom management.

Adrian Liberty and Henry Flocken (who formally changed his name to Giniw-giizhig) started taking Earl Nyholm's Ojibwe classes at Bemidji State University when I was still early in my efforts there, and we soon became fast friends. We sang together at powwows and eventually on ceremonial drums, growing into that spiritual space while our language efforts deepened as individuals. A few years later, Adrian Liberty and Leslie Harper started Niigaane, the tribal-language-medium program at the Bug-O-Nay-Ge-Shig School on the Leech Lake Reservation, another Ojibwe-medium school, which immediately took off with great community support.

In 1994, I got a call from Isadore Toulouse, a great speaker of Eastern Ojibwe, who invited me to speak at the inaugural Anishinaabemowin Teg language conference in Sault Ste. Marie. I have attended for most of the last twenty-five years now. Isadore came to see us often in Minnesota. That Ojibwe language conference he built grew from one hundred attendees to over one thousand, making a major impact on language program development throughout Ontario and Michigan.

The number of my friends and colleagues in the emerging Ojibwe language-revitalization arena grew, but we often worked alone. Each of us had mentors, and while we sometimes worked with the same people—Jim Clark, Nancy Jones, Eugene Stillday, and Anna Gibbs come to mind—we often went in our own directions. Nobody was tethered or restrained. Sometimes we worked in enclaves or small groups. The tribal-language-medium schools were especially demanding. The staff had to be curriculum writers, administrators, and teachers, all full time and all at the same time. That was productive but sometimes isolating.

To fight this, we sometimes got together. We had a large language camp on the campus of the Bug-O-Nay-Ge-Shig School, and I was so pleased to use my influence with the staff to get most of these young language warriors employed there, along with twenty fluent elders and lots of young learners. Rick Gresczyk, who is non-Native but was raised as a fluent speaker by Maude Kegg, joined us. Doris and Lorraine White

Crow, Hartley White, Porky White, Murphy Thomas, and many other great speakers were there. We got up at five every morning and worked only in Ojibwe. I think the elders were excited to see capable young leadership eager to learn what they knew. And for me and many of the other younger folks there, we were hungry for the language and the connections with our elders, but for one another as well. We started hatching plans. In true Ojibwe fashion, we didn't do everything together or in the same places, and nobody could claim credit for anyone else's inspiration or effort. But the water was flowing in the right direction.

When Archie died and I assumed leadership responsibilities in the ceremonial world, most of the new language warriors started to come to Round Lake. At first, like Archie, I had to do all the talks and sing all the songs. But I recruited, supported, and conscientiously trained in new people. Keller Paap was one of the first I recruited to work as an Oshkaabewis (Messenger) there. After fifteen years assisting in that capacity, Keller has now graduated to a chief at Round Lake, and shares half of the initiation work with me. There are now at least one hundred people who sing the songs there, and several who can do most of the talks. It was heartening to see people younger than us stepping up, not just as students but as leaders in the effort as well. This happened at ceremony and in the academic world. Two of John Nichols's graduate students—Brendan Fairbanks and Michael Sullivan—really excelled and are now PhD–carrying, book-publishing, skilled and knowledgeable teachers of the language.

*   *   *

I think most people recognize that when the natural, intergenerational transmission of a language breaks down, the language is in trouble. If kids are not learning the target language as their first language in the home, your entire population has to rely on something else—schools, programs, and universities—to advance the language. And none of those places get as much time with young learners as their families do, at home. Focusing on developing language skills in children makes a lot of sense for many reasons. Their brains are ready for this kind of learning. The sooner they learn, the greater the longevity of their learning curve and ability to use what they learn. It's easier to keep kids in a target-language-rich learning environment than it is to keep adults there. But getting started is really hard if your language is at the point where most of your speakers are elders with no teaching degrees or classroom management or curriculum development training.

Several young second-language learners came up with a great idea to address the shortage of successful young adult second-language learners. Lucia Bonacci, Michelle Goose, Persia Erdrich, and others wanted to see an immersion opportunity for adult learners—something intense, productive, and truly immersive. Too often, language camps degenerated into English-language-sharing circles because target-language discipline broke down. Organizers, out of kindness, wanted to appease attendees' desire for comfort, rather than focus on the rigor of serious language learning. Often it was the great speakers themselves who broke discipline, frustrated with students who had limited capacity to understand them. You can only talk *at* someone for so long when you are acclimated to conversing *with* people whenever you want. These young language warriors formed an organization, Ojibwemotaadidaa Omaa Gidakiiminaang (OOG). They hunted for funding and have received sustainable support from the Fond du Lac Band of Ojibwe. They set up a fluent-speaker-to-student ratio of around one-to-one in an adult immersion program. They have experimented with several different formats, but usually students commit to an intensive, three-week summer program and one weekend per month for a year. Students must apply, and they are interviewed in Ojibwe as part of the application process. This eliminates students who have limited ability to withstand a genuine immersion environment. It's for students with some solid language building blocks already in place. Once accepted, students agree not to bring cell phones into the program or classroom environments, not to use English, and to attend all scheduled sessions. While this makes the program hard for students who have children, demanding jobs, or limited Ojibwe experience, the results are stunning. Every accepted student grows to fluency quickly, and almost all of them find gainful employment in tribal-language-medium schools and other Ojibwe learning environments.

There are 250,000 Ojibwe people in the United States and Canada, and many of them want genuine language programming in their communities. Some of the tribes and First Nations are willing to get behind such efforts. The biggest roadblock for many of them is the lack of qualified Ojibwe teachers. OOG is helping to build more successful second-language learners, and most of their students are eager young adults who are hungry for their language and culture. Lakehead University in Thunder Bay, Ontario, also has a program designed to take fluent speakers of Ojibwe and equip them with credentials, classroom management skills, and curricular acumen and launch them into this work. They've been at it for decades and have greatly enabled the Ojibwe language work going on in Canada today. Now, there are Ojibwe-medium programs starting for early childhood and some of the early grades in several different places. Some are even in urban areas—there is one in Duluth, and another in Minneapolis that houses both Ojibwe and Dakota programs. Red Lake is also trying hard to get into the Ojibwe-medium-education game, and their preschool program, Waasabiik Ojibwemotaadiwin Immersion School, is off to a good start.

Every single emerging program and effort has growing pains. Those in Ojibwe country all say they need more target-language-competent (TL-competent) staff. The ability of those who have launched OOG and some of the university programs to train TL-competent teachers has the potential to make or break this movement. If they fail to scale up the delivery of more teachers, they force the Ojibwe-medium school expansion to slow, stall, or plateau for a long time. But if they can get it right and start really producing, they can uncork more Ojibwe-medium school expansion, from elementary all the way through high school and beyond, and in more communities.

There also are huge barriers for university language-program growth. Most universities have the attitude that if you can make them come, *then* they will build it. They rarely have an attitude that says, let's build it and then they will come. TL-teaching programs have to justify their existence before they can exist. There isn't a huge philanthropic resource pool they can tap, either. Most of the really successful tribes, such as the Shakopee Mdewakanton Sioux Community, which donates around $42 million every year, give their assets to infrastructure projects requested by other tribes rather than to endowments of non-Native institutions or to program funds. And a university program will need staff sustainably financed for many years to really bear fruit. While this is discouraging, it does not have to terminate the dream. Even the Hawaiians, who have no federal recognition as a Native nation, found ways to develop these programs through a combination of grants, institutional support, and other fund-raising. This is a critical piece of the work. A mature, functional, naturally growing language revitalization effort will deliver at the community level; at the elementary, middle, and high school levels; at the university level; and across multiple venues—schools, programs, publications, the internet, and technological operating systems.

* * *

It is critically important to set the right tone for your work. Take every facet of the effort seriously. Your community probably does have at least an interest in seeing something happen with the language. Your first forays into the effort have to engage those folks. People often are intimidated by the thought of learning a language. They don't want to expose their ignorance. We have shame issues in our communities, and nobody wants to be accused of not being Native enough by an eager, young language warrior. And the older people are, the more likely they are to have a hard time confessing to the limitations of their own knowledge. Be kind. Be generous. Be encouraging. When children take their first steps and stumble, we don't shout them down, tell them it wasn't good enough, or laugh. We encourage. And they try some more.

At the same time that community language efforts need to be fun and encouraging, they also need to be productive. If you want a language-enrichment experience, that's a fine goal. Be explicit about what it is. Don't call it an immersion camp if you intend only to provide a little grammar or vocabulary lesson while everyone is immersed in English. But if you want to do a bona fide immersion camp, immerse the students. Establish expectations for target-language discipline for everyone there and stick to it.

You have to grow your team. Use a strengths-based approach to the work. Some people have passion or skill for different parts of the work. The Cherokee, Maori, and Hawaiians have been very clever about this. Some people focused on lexical expansion—new words for firewall, internet portal, modem, fiduciary responsibility, algebraic formula, and so forth. Some took responsibility for elementary teaching. Some took responsibility for administrative work, fund-raising, and organizing. Others worked the politics. This makes practical sense. It also sets a tone of inclusion. Even those who have limited language skills but truly value your effort can be put to work in fund-raising and organizational work, sharing the load and building the movement.

*   *   *

I am an academic, so I see the irony in making the next point: beware of academics. The anthropologists, historians, and linguists are interested in our people, but the reasons for their interest are different from ours. While all see fruit for academic inquiry in our spaces, they are trying to advance their careers and publish books. That doesn't mean they are only self-serving. Many have genuine relationships with Native people on the ground and don't leave them as nameless informants for their work. John Nichols, who has done incredible work as a linguist, has been especially generous in crediting his Native sources, and even refuses to accept royalty payments on his books, sending it all to the Kegg family in Mille Lacs, in honor of his many years working with Maude Kegg and the books she made possible. But our people have been ripped off in a thousand different ways over the years, and our intellectual, cultural, and linguistic property is no different.

Use linguists and other academics. They know things. They have credentials. They can be helpful with grants. They can help get you published. Their support can add to our efforts. Just don't be used by them. Stay in control. Be informed about copyrights, royalties, pricing, and the use of products they help produce. When all that is sorted out, academics can catalyze our efforts. And they can be great friends.

Use linguists and academics, but don't surrender control to them or rely on them to revitalize our languages or cultures. They are linguistic recorders, not cultural carriers. They can build capacity and launch and sustain vital projects. But they don't talk, move, act, or believe like Indigenous people, so you still have to have our people in front of the kids. If we fail to do this, we can inadvertently enable or create a Jesus complex in the center of our language work: people will feel like they need a white savior instead of an indigenous empowerment program. I use that analogy with full knowledge of the irony that many people actually think Jesus looked white because there is a normalized vision of a Nordic Jesus in half the houses in North America, when he was actually a Semite from the Middle East, as brown as any Native American.

* * *

There are many tools out there, but no silver bullets. The master-apprentice model of language learning has gotten a lot of attention. Leanne Hinton and other language activists and scholars have written about the method. The idea is simple: pair up a master—a great, fluent speaker—with an apprentice—an eager, second-language learner. Arrange to have them spend a significant amount of time together, structure the time enough to maintain target-language discipline but not so much as to seem or be prescriptive. In some ways, without any structure or formality, this is what I did with Archie Mosay. Some tribes, like the Ho-Chunk in Wisconsin, have funded and employed this model with significant success. When done right, the master-apprentice model can build deep, lasting relationships that have the potential to reestablish intergenerational transmission of language within the dyad. It can be a powerful language-learning-and-teaching strategy and very healing for both student and teacher to be so validated. That's what happens when it's done right.

Unfortunately, it's really hard to do the master-apprentice programs right. Both the master and the apprentice have to be deeply committed to one another and to the effort. Discipline breaks down everywhere, not just at language camps. The grandchildren of the master parade through learning space, operating in English. The phone rings. English. The radio goes off. English. The television is on. English. The apprentices lose discipline because they get distracted or want a shortcut to higher-level grammar concepts and don't know how to ask without speaking English. People fall in love. They get lazy. Life happens. And that's for the truly committed. If the master-apprentice model is applied on a large scale, it amplifies the problems. Let's say a tribe decides to fund a program for twelve masters paired with twelve apprentices. They agree to a certain number of hours for immersion per week and start paying everyone. Money makes people funny. Now the check is expected and relied upon. People get cranky if something threatens the money. They also get complacent. The staying power to keep at it, month after month, gets taxed. Then people skip some time here and there, or decide to take a break and bring the master to bingo instead of talking in the target language. Then you have to hire someone to check on everyone to make sure they are doing what was agreed. Then you have young people trying to police their elders on language discipline, and you get problems. Again, it works if it's done right, and it doesn't if it's not. And it's hard to mitigate the risks. It is worth a try if you can gather committed masters and apprentices and really stick to your guns.

Rosetta Stone, Duolingo, Babbel, Pimsleur, and other established online language-learning companies have done exhaustive studies of human cognition and language learning. According to Pimsleur, if a person hears a new word, they forget it after five seconds. If they hear it again after five seconds, they remember it for thirty. If they hear a word at intervals of one, five, and thirty seconds, they can remember it for half an hour. So they designed a system of repetitions and reinforcements to make their naturally flowing lessons more effective. We now have elementary Ojibwe on Pimsleur, and it's great. There are male and female speakers from different communities who are first speakers, and lessons produce results. I use Pimsleur in my classes at Bemidji State University. But it's not perfect. It can't encompass all dialects. We don't have intermediate and advanced Ojibwe yet. The start-up capital required for any such undertaking is significant. Some of the money pays for the recording studio, the sound and video engineers, the language people who will populate the program, and the company's profit. It's worth it. It just takes a huge investment of time and money.

Stephen Greymorning has another system for vocabulary building that can add to other efforts and has gained traction in some language spaces. It is mainly a cognition-based vocabulary pyramid that can be scaled up for some basic grammar development. He is the first to say that the system is not a replacement for sound, well-rounded programming, tribal-language-medium schools, and other efforts. It is not a silver bullet. But it is worth a look. Some levers can help with curriculum and program development, but there are no shortcuts to daily discipline.

* * *

Building your leadership team requires a conscientious and sustained effort. I learned my lessons about leadership development primarily through personal experience. As I have transitioned from eager student of our language and ways to someone who is called upon to do a lot of teaching, speaking, and leading in both realms, I am always humbled by the memory of my great mentors. I can never replace them in any capacity, but I have no choice but to succeed them in some. Although I am careful not to beat myself up or run myself down about my shortcomings of knowledge or character, they are plainly obvious to me. I am always brimming with gratitude for all my mentors have given me, and I work hard to shoulder the trust they placed in me and many others to keep their words and work alive. I keep Mary Roberts's teaching close: take everything you learn and teach it to at least four other people. If you know one word, teach it to four others. If you learn a ceremony, don't just do the ceremony; take the time to teach it to at least four others. We should endeavor to make ourselves replaceable many times over.

I learned a lot about working well with others the hard way, and I surely have more to learn. Our Medicine Dance is an especially complicated ceremony, with very long legends, complicated song repertoires, detailed procedures, and lots of people who need patient coaching, guidance, and help. To lead such a ceremony requires gifts with music, language, and people. It requires integrity and reliability and lots of hard work. Nobody wishes to be chief unless they don't know what being chief entails.

Building people up takes time. Sometimes people have a great gift in connecting with others but don't know their languages. Sometimes people know their language but they have dark clouds of negativity following them everywhere they go.

It is easiest to maximize people's contributions by really connecting with them, learning what they want to contribute, and finding out what their greatest strengths are. People need to start with their strengths. Over time, they can build more well-rounded sets of skills for more difficult leadership positions. Pay close attention to what people can handle. Sometimes someone has great potential but needs to be protected from being overwhelmed by the work. I try to insulate people I first bring into the work from some of the pressure so they can raise young children and develop their careers. Then as they become ready to shoulder more of the work, I let them lean into it. Others are overeager and need to be slowed down, grounded, and guided without dampening their enthusiasm and passion. When I lead, I try to stand up for my team, protect them, and also free them to take on as much as they can. I haven't handled things perfectly, but I know there are many dedicated people with whom I have worked for years who might have burned out or stepped away if I hadn't been attentive to these things.

A growing language-revitalization effort requires the same attentive development of leaders and team members. You must have one another's backs. Gossip, backbiting, lateral oppression, and crabs-in-the-bucket stuff can be death blows to your team's cohesiveness and the stability of the work, even in established language spaces. Pay attention to one another's needs. You need each other. Nobody is replaceable. That does not mean that toxic behavior or a toxic person should be tolerated or given a pass. It does mean that nobody can afford to be self-absorbed. Think of the big picture, the language goals you have set for your community, the babies you want to be leading us after you are gone. That will help you keep perspective and stay patient when things get hard. And they will get hard.

Remember to tend to your own engagement. We all get tired

and burned out from time to time. Everyone is wired differ-
ently. Find out what recharges you and do it in abundance. At
our drum ceremonies, we tell people that warriors have to be in
charge of leading the people to peace. That makes perfect sense.

Every major effort, every job, every relationship comes with
a crap sandwich. You will get tired. You will get tired of being
tired. You will have a small group of leaders that you will never
get a break from. Take a deep breath. An episode of the television series *Scrubs* provides the perfect metaphor: "Grab the
crap sandwich, put a pickle on top, and take a big bite."[7] Smile.
Repeat. And your language will live.

*   *   *

While there are no quick fixes, many tools already exist that
can greatly catalyze your efforts. You have to spend a little
time developing a shared understanding with your team about
which tools you want to embrace. When you do, the power can
be stunning.

New technologies offer some of the greatest opportunities
for expansive growth. I have already mentioned a few ways
technology can help, but there are more. I understand that most
of our elders did not learn their languages using the internet or
cell phone apps. But they also did not have the internet or cell-
phone apps pulling them away from their language. Most tribal
people today are modern. They use phones and computers. We
have to get those things to speak our languages, or our people
will be speaking English.

These technologies have the power to overcome two of the
biggest obstacles to language revitalization—time and space.
One precious speaker never has enough time to do all the teaching and coaching, but when we record that speaker and share
his or her words through various technological applications,

they can teach for hundreds of years. Many of our people cannot travel to places where the language is used. Half of the tribal population lives in urban areas that are dominated by English. The reservations are dominated by English too. Finding real language enclaves and nests is hard. But when we open up a computer, we can transport ourselves into some of those spaces more easily, which can help bridge gaps in learning opportunities and expand the work.

Several years ago, I was asked to speak at the Indigenous Language Institute (ILI). They gathered people from many communities where innovative work was happening with tribal languages. I met Joe Erb, a language warrior at the center of Cherokee language revitalization in Oklahoma, and I was amazed by his demonstration. With language folks from all over the United States and Canada sitting in the conference room, he opened up Skype and connected to the Cherokee-medium classroom in Tahlequah, Oklahoma. He spoke to the kids in Cherokee, and they gave an enthusiastic response, also in Cherokee. He spoke to the audience about the diaspora of the Cherokee people and their work to revitalize Cherokee. Then he connected to the Cherokee-medium program in North Carolina, also via Skype. Soon he had the kids in North Carolina and the kids in Oklahoma speaking to one another and singing songs together, while a room full of language warriors gathered in New Mexico and smiled.

While Skype was new then, it's almost primitive today compared to the technologies of our time—which will soon look outdated. I routinely deliver my classes interactively from Bemidji, which is located in northern Minnesota, to Onamia, in central Minnesota; to Mankato, in southern Minnesota; and to other locations. Cisco and other big technology companies have created customized, interactive-technology spaces that are even more impressive. I saw a demonstration involving customized rooms built on two separate sites, each shaped like a half circle. With the touch of a button, the rooms appeared to connect, and it felt and looked like everyone was sitting in the same circular room. The sound was directional, seeming to come from each speaker. Cameras did not have to be repositioned. We were in the same space, even though we were hundreds of miles apart. This type of technology will only grow better and more sophisticated. Some of it is inexpensive, like Skype, while some is really expensive, like Cisco's customized tech rooms. But all of it can contribute to a major language revitalization effort. We cannot live in a modern world and hold ourselves hostage to wigwam technology, pretending that we will win the fight to keep our languages alive. I build wigwams every summer and use them for ceremonial and social purposes. But I make use of the best technology I can find to keep our academic, political, and financial footings for language revitalization as strong as possible.

Many tribes have communities in several different states and provinces. Use the technology to open space for knowledge-sharing and cooperative work. Blackfeet, Ojibwe, Cree, Potawatomi, Ho-Chunk, Lakota, Cherokee, Oneida, Salish, Seminole, and many other groups can greatly benefit from an effort to work together across space, rather than try to reinvent the wheel in every one of the many spaces where their people live.

I get multiple emails every day asking for Ojibwe language materials, recordings, charts, and learning opportunities. Trying to keep up with all of the queries was exhausting. So I worked with the web team at Bemidji State University to create a web-based clearinghouse for links and connections and resources. It's not perfect or comprehensive, but it's a great place to get people started. It lists language tables, university programs, books, resources, and contacts. Now when I get queries, I send them a link.

For years I have edited the *Oshkaabewis Native Journal*, which remains the only academic journal of the Ojibwe language. A few years ago, we wrote a grant that enabled us to set up all of the journal's back issues with a print-on-demand publishing service with ISBN and Amazon listings. We then put PDFs of all back issues on the website at Bemidji State University, available free, along with all audio recordings. For this particular publication, we felt that any revenue generated through back-issue sales would be relatively small. What we really wanted to do was maximize access for our people, many of whom struggle financially. It provided a real boost to access to the language material. The word *free* sounds great in every language.

We use the radio, Vimeo and YouTube, video shorts on Facebook, and other venues to promote and normalize use of Ojibwe. Many people have made this a big part of what they do. For example, James Vukelich, a high school teacher in the Twin Cities, posts an Ojibwe word or phrase of the day on Facebook, an activity that has taken on a life of its own. These types of contributions often have high visibility and can amplify efforts elsewhere. They also create more familiar and comfortable access for many people who worry about being shamed or judged for what they don't know. In addition, short language pieces don't require perfect fluency, and this creates an avenue where good second-language learners can contribute meaningfully beyond their role as great students.

Video documentaries developed about the revitalization of Hawaiian, Ojibwe, and Blackfoot have been instrumental in raising awareness about what is working, what is not working, and who is doing the work. These can bring new awareness of the issues and show people why they should care, which can translate into support for political objectives and academic program development. Apathy is the enemy of momentum, and we need to develop momentum. This kind of work can help break through distrust in both Native and non-Native circles. It can also help with fund-raising. In 2010, Twin Cities Public Television developed a documentary on Ojibwe revitalization called *First Speakers: Restoring the Ojibwe Language*. It won a regional Emmy Award, still runs once or twice a year, and is available online. That by itself doesn't revitalize the language. But it amplifies the message in places that can meaningfully contribute to the work in the trenches. It's also a healthy way to engage white allies. They can't revitalize Ojibwe for us, but they can help catalyze our efforts and develop important relationships to magnify the impact of what we do.

Technology can connect people, places, information, and ideas; that is its special power. But without the people, places, information, and ideas to connect, it will only create the illusion of effort rather than meaningful change. Be honest with yourselves about what you need. Don't develop blind spots or count on any single resource—be that a person, a school, or a new technology. There is no savior for this kind of work. There is just the work. Give it everything you have.

* * *

For teaching Ojibwe and most other tribal languages, we were, and remain, in dire need of new resources. The accelerated-reader programs used for English in most grade schools have more than five thousand books available, carefully developed for each phase of reading development: sight words, basic sentences, paragraph books, and chapter books. Often a child comes into kindergarten not knowing letters, yet by second grade, some kids are reading *Harry Potter*. It's a stunning learning curve. If we don't even have the books, much less all the tools for teaching literacy, or the assessments and computer support for testing the kids, we won't advance this critical literacy goal in any language. That's unacceptable. But we can't just teach English literacy and forget about our languages. That's also unacceptable. We need to develop our own books and our own ecosystem for literacy development in our languages.

Developing books is hard. Every one of the Ojibwe-medium schools started the process by translating English picture books and taping Ojibwe text over the English words, which is allowed under copyright law. But those books could not be sold or distributed, and the material did not translate well. In books of Mother Goose rhymes, for example, we were cramming Ojibwe words into English thought patterns. All the characters were white. Even the animals were not indigenous to our area or representative of our clans. The morals and lessons also were based in a different culture. Yes, we can all learn something from "The Little Red Hen." But the lesson that makes sense for developing a work ethic—don't share unless others pitch in—undermines the communal sharing of harvests prominent in many Native cultures. We didn't want to add our voices to those who were trying to teach our kids to be white—something they could never be accepted as being and something that would never feed their knowledge of self, empowerment, or sense of belonging. We had to do more, and that meant we had to do it ourselves.

The power of relationships came to bear as we rolled out one of our first major literacy resource initiatives. I had done a lot of work with the Minnesota Humanities Center (MHC) in the areas of teacher training, cultural competency, racial equity, and other indigenous educational efforts. In 2008, the MHC had a small pot of money and an interest in advancing some of the growing indigenous-language work in Minnesota. After a series of conversations with Matthew Brandt and others at the MHC, I contacted Keller Paap and Adrian Liberty to plan a process for several knowledgeable first speakers of Ojibwe and several advanced, second-language learners of Ojibwe to develop a young-reader series, monolingual in Ojibwe.

I was tasked with putting the working group together, so I approached the entire effort with reckless ambition and a healthy dose of naïveté. I brought in nine great first speakers, elders I considered to be our Jedi-masters of the Ojibwe language. I also invited staff from the two Ojibwe-medium schools operating in our region at the time. The MHC paid modest travel stipends to participants and kept them fed. I thought that if we just locked everyone in a room, it would be easy to develop new stories, but I was wrong. These established storytellers did not feel comfortable developing new material. They could tell stories they already heard all day long. But it is taboo to tell our winter legends out of season, and we were committed to observing traditional protocols. They could also talk about their own lived experiences and childhood memories. But we really wanted to develop kids' books that were age appropriate and engaging. I was hoping that we could develop characters that were animals indigenous to our area and use an indigenous, Ojibwe-focused cultural tapestry for the telling of modern and relatable stories. We had to start everything from scratch.

I finally broke through by focusing on what was comfortable for the elders and developing storyboards collectively. It went like this: I asked Nancy Jones, the esteemed elder from Ontario, to talk about her childhood memories. She told us that whenever she was naughty she got sent to her grandmother's house.

Her grandmother would boss her around in Ojibwe: "Fetch wood. Build a fire. Wash the dishes. Mop the floor."

"Then what happened?" I asked.

"I got sent to the other grandma's house and did the same thing all over again."

She also said that whenever she finished a chore session, her grandma would touch her white hair and then run her hand across Nancy's head and say, "Waabikwaan bezhig gimiinin. (I'm giving you a white hair.)" The message was deeper than it sounds: Because age is so respected in Ojibwe culture and longevity is prized over looking young, telling someone that they have just earned a white hair is a blessing. It says you get to be an elder, too, someday. You'll earn your right to be an elder one good deed at a time.

Then I spoke to the assembled team. I told them that what we really wanted with these stories was something like what Nancy had shared—a deep grounding in our culture, our values, our ways of doing things. But I said it would be even more relatable if we modernized the setting and picked a cast of characters, maybe animals and birds that represented our clans, and had each show attributes of those clans. We started to develop characters and storyboards. For Nancy's first story, we picked Migiziins (Little Eagle) and set the bird up in a modern house with tables and chairs. I was imagining something like the television shows *Franklin* or *Little Bear*. I asked Nancy to imagine Migiziins coming to the table for breakfast and eating corn flakes.

She was able to jump right in, "And listening to his iPod."

I said, "Exactly. And then what happens?"

"His mom sends him to grandma's house."

Next, we went through the chores he would do. And then, "Waabikwaan bezhig gimiinin," of course giving the eagle a white feather instead of a white hair. We had Migiziins go home, hip-hopping down the road to the tunes on his iPod while the little birds shook their heads at him, then pouting to his mom, who had him look in the mirror. It takes an eagle seven years for its brown head feathers to turn white, so as he looked in the mirror and saw his first white feather, a smile came across his face. That scenario began as a storyboard. Then we took that outline—indigenous in origin, loaded with Ojibwe values, infused with indigenous characters and settings but modern and relatable—and we had Nancy tell the story from her outline. I recorded the story session and we went through it, line by line, to make sure I had captured her words in her way. We developed a list of illustrations and got the artists, who were also at the session, cranking on the art.

We found our rhythm. We developed storyboards together and then broke out into small groups, with an elder speaker anchoring each one. Each group produced a story. Then we brought all the stories into the large group to share and seek advice and feedback on framing and language use. This way, each speaker was in charge of his or her own stories. Each story had a dialect determined by the speaker. But all dialects were able to go in the same book without changing any of them. All storytellers benefitted from feedback on the creative and linguistic elements of their work without being disempowered in its production. In three days, we developed thirty stories and proofread them. The artists could not keep up with our elders. I spent the next several months editing, double-checking everything with John Nichols and other experienced linguists, pressing the artists, and developing the layouts.

As the work took shape, we arranged for publication monolingually in Ojibwe with Wiigwaas Press. Heid Erdrich developed that press with the express intention of producing indigenous-language books. We had a follow-up session and doubled the amount of produced work. Now there are four books in the series and more yet to be published. The first, *Awesiinyensag: Dibaajimowinan Ji-gikinoo'amaageng*, won a major award as Best Read from the Center for the Book at the Library of Congress. The biggest accolade I heard for it, however, came during a site visit I did at Waadookodaading Ojibwe Language Institute in Reserve, Wisconsin, shortly after the book was released. One of the second graders came running up to me, gushing in Ojibwe, "Howah! Niminwendaan iw mazina'igan *Awesiiyensag* gaa-agindamaan. Baapinendaagwad. (Wow! I really like that book *Awesiiyensag* that I read. It's funny.)" The book did what books are supposed to do: it took the work and words of our elders and put them in the brain of a young child living hundreds of miles away from where the stories were told. And it all happened without any translations or use of English. It helped him learn, and it entertained along the way.*

*   *   *

---

*We have since developed an agreement to move the books to the Minnesota Historical Society Press, where they will benefit from more comprehensive marketing and the ability to stay in print much longer. And in 2019, the Mille Lacs Band of Ojibwe began a major Ojibwe-language resource-development initiative. I was asked to coordinate the initiative's first-language book-development effort. The tribe identified twenty-two fluent first speakers who wanted to work on language books. The staff at their Aanjibimaadizing program coordinated food and facilities, and we brought in all of the available speakers they identified, each paired up with a transcriber, plus linguists and artists. Our first session produced 150 pages of Ojibwe text in fifty stories. We plan to do three such sessions every year for the foreseeable future and publish books for all reading levels.

We learned a lot from the book development experiences and took the lessons into other parts of the work as well. One of the other major needs we have is for lexical expansion—new vocabulary for new technologies and even non-Native concepts that we needed to teach about in the tribal-language-medium schools. Most charters for the tribal-language-medium schools say that they will meet state or provincial educational standards, but that they will do so in their respective tribal languages. As a result, we needed to develop a way to talk about and teach a variety of subjects and topics: algebra, *Robert's Rules of Order*, filibuster, soil percolation, and many others. Ultimately, we want our kids to be successful mathematicians, politicians, lawyers, business owners, and scientists, as well as lodge chiefs, drum chiefs, Ojibwe professors, and elementary school teachers.

In 2009, I assembled many of the same team members we had used on the first literacy projects. Again, my naïveté and ambition caused us to both stumble and excel. I thought if I just got the Jedi masters of Ojibwe together in the same room, they would have no trouble developing new vocabulary. They never seemed to be at a loss for words. And surely they could see the importance of such an effort—or so I thought. When we were assembled for the first such session, one of the venerable Ojibwe speakers from Ponemah, Eugene Stillday, challenged me about the very objective of our work: "Why do we need to do this? Algebra? I don't know what algebra means in any language and I don't care. Teach our kids who we are." I was aware that some of the academic areas of the lexicon expansion would stretch our elders—it was out of their comfort zone and daily-knowledge base. But I truly believed they had it in them. I pushed back: "Eugene, across the ocean in China there are a billion people learning algebra. And it does not reduce their Chineseness because they are doing the learning in Chinese. These concepts can be taught in any language. We just need the words. If we don't lean into this and find the words, remember that our kids learning algebra is compulsory. We will doom them to learning it in English." He stared at me for a minute. Then he said, "Okay. I will help you. But I still don't know what algebra means in any language." We all laughed. And then we got started.

Now the beauty of having a diverse team of first speakers really paid off. Gordon Jourdain was raised by monolingual Ojibwe-speaking grandparents. As a young man he worked on a roofing crew that spoke Ojibwe, so he already had vocabulary for words like *pitch*, *angle*, *square footage*, and other related terminology. He could even take the square root of the hypotenuse in Ojibwe. But for most of the other great first speakers, this was new material. Gordon was able to help cross-pollinate their existing knowledge with his. By himself, Eugene might not have had a word for *right angle*, but when he heard Gordon's word, he could say, "I understand that. Here's how we'd say that where I come from." Instead of picking one correct word or dialect, we documented all variances. Where one speaker diverged from another, we included both words in the lexicon and noted the speaker by initials next to each entry. There was variation, but less than many people might expect. The speakers often agreed about new terminology.

We also found that trying to explain complex philosophical or abstract ideas and seek translations for them was less productive than taking a more practical approach. For example, when we had science terminology, we projected pictures of environmental and scientific processes on the wall. With a second overhead projector, we started typing up the brainstorming process and the word lists. Everyone provided feedback, asked questions, and expanded the conversation on morphology. In one case, we wanted terminology on condensation. Many of the speakers didn't know what the word *condensation* meant in English, so we put up pictures. Anna Gibbs said, "Oh, you mean like when the water comes together, like on the grass. That's *abwese*." Her sister, Rose Tainter, said, "Yeah, but when you're parked at the drive-in movie theater and it gets wet on the inside of the windshield, that's *abweyaabikad*." They started ping-ponging words around. There is not *a* word for condensation in Ojibwe; there are about twenty words, different ones for different textures and forms, animate or inanimate: *abwebiig* (the noun for condensation), *abwese* (to condense on an object), *abwe-ayaamagad* (to condense in air), *abwebiigad* (to condense on fabric), *abweyaabikad* (to condense on glass or metal), and more. Getting to the heart of the morphemes (the smallest meaningful parts of words) was the key to uncorking real accomplishment for everyone. Keller Paap and I took notes all day and then stayed up until two in the morning each night, typing and editing. The elders worked hard all day, from about eight in the morning until eight at night. When they got up the morning of the second day we had a one-hundred-page word list waiting for them. We spent lots of time double-checking everything in groups and taking the conversation to new areas. Sometimes the elders melted down and went off on a tangent (we documented, for example, about thirty words for different kinds of farting). We put in a lot of hard work, and we got a lot of laughs and two new dictionaries out of the effort: *Aaniin Ekidong: Ojibwe Vocabulary Project* and *Ezhichigeyang: Ojibwe Word List*.

* * *

In the Ojibwe world, a new marriage between age-old linguistic practices and modern technology revolutionized our efforts. Any healthy language-revitalization effort has to be bigger than one person, one school, one small niche group of die-hards. It has to grow. And people have to be able to find ways to contribute that are meaningful to them as well as to the larger effort. We have tried to support language learners eager to help with simple books, and we have also encouraged and tried to include non-Native linguists who are equipped and motivated to add to the effort. Our languages are part of our identity as Native people. But it means a lot to many people outside our communities when we find ways to thrive and when they find ways to help make that possible. We should never look to whites to save us; the only sensible approach is to utilize *everyone's* work.

In the Ojibwe language universe, non-Native linguists like John Nichols and Rand Valentine have immeasurably added to our efforts. They are sincere, humble, hardworking, and deeply knowledgeable. Nichols in particular was deeply involved in our literacy and vocabulary projects. He spent decades working with Maude Kegg from Mille Lacs. When she passed away in the mid-1990s, he lost a dear friend and a professional connection that drove a lot of his work. I brought him around our area and introduced him to Eugene Stillday, Marlene Stately, Leona Wakanabo, Anna Gibbs, Leonard Moose, and many others. Eventually those connections started to feed his work— although everything they accomplished was their own work entirely.

Recognizing the power of new technology and the need to work across dialects, Nichols created the Ojibwe People's Dictionary (OPD), which is housed at, and supported by the faculty and students in, the Department of American Indian Studies at the University of Minnesota. It is a web-based dictionary, free to access, that includes entries from multiple dialects. The word lists there grow every day. Words can be sorted by morpheme. And almost all entries have audio. You can go to an entry, pick the dialect you want to hear, select a male or female speaker, and then hear the word in clips from naturally recorded speech. You can also read and hear sample sentences. It's quite brilliant. The content there is now synced with the online catalog of objects in the Minnesota Historical Society (MNHS). If you look up *bandolier bag*, for example, you can see authentic bandolier bags and links to the material culture of the Ojibwe in the MNHS archives. With every new project we embark on, John circles back to the speakers to record the new vocabulary and use it to expand the lists on the OPD, which is already larger than the largest print dictionary for the language. This is not Wikipedia for Ojibwe, where anyone can add entries. All entries have to be vetted by the team and recorded and carefully managed, so it takes tremendous work to maintain and grow the dictionary. It has been a monumental contribution to the language.

Charles Lippert manages another dictionary resource for Ojibwe. Unlike the OPD, Freelang's Ojibwe dictionary (which is also online only and free to use) allows entries from multiple sources and does not try to standardize writing systems or spelling. It's similar to Wikipedia for authorship and editing, although it's dictionary-like in format—just word lists. While it has some dialect filters, it is full of inconsistencies that make it hard for a beginning Ojibwe student to use it. But many of us who are more deeply involved in language-revitalization work use it often because Lippert has been so great about adding new material all the time. It's the best place to go when looking for ideas to start a vocabulary-expansion conversation or hunt for rare words. Freelang is therefore a real contributor, but whatever you find there still has to be vetted by someone who knows his or her stuff.

*   *   *

As you create materials that work for you, or look for projects to take on, you may want to add to the materials that are available in print and digitally. After all, once something is built or published, it can be used again and again. The Hawaiians had such a rich literary tradition and numerous magazines published when the entire population was fluent that even today they have yet to mine everything for dictionary development. Jon Fila, an educational leader in one of the Twin Cities' public schools, has a novel idea. Minnesota school districts, like many others across the country, have been frustrated by the quality of textbooks that are available. The big commercial publishers produce only textbooks that will be adopted, statewide, by large states: in effect, Minnesotans are forced to purchase textbooks made in Texas by Texans for Texans. Fila wants to develop thousands of regionally and culturally competent and appropriate lesson plans and curricular modules, with Minnesota educators for Minnesota educators. And he wants to publish everything online with a Creative Commons license, meaning that anybody can copy, download, and use the material for free. If he succeeds, not only will Minnesota's school districts not have to buy materials from Texas; they won't have to buy materials, period. That would save every district millions of dollars that can then be spent on other things central to their mission. It would be a win for districts, a win for students, a win for teachers, and a win for taxpayers. An initiative like this is not without trade-offs, because quality management and reliability of the resources and the technological support for their use and access are critical and not always certain. But the potential of this undertaking is obvious. Although Fila's idea is broad and goes beyond a language-specific focus, he is very interested in working with Minnesota's indigenous languages too. By putting in some time up front, we could develop a reliable series of tools adaptable by any district in the state that wants to offer some tribal-language teaching to its students. That's powerful leverage and worth a serious look.

Major digital projects offer other ways to bring the language to learners and speakers. Hawaiian, Navajo, Cherokee, and a couple other tribal language groups have worked on producing target-language versions of the operating systems for Apple and Microsoft. The companies are willing to do their part. They want everyone using their stuff. Do not underestimate the scope of this undertaking: the Microsoft operating system requires two hundred thousand translations. But once it is done, it transfers into each new iteration of the software. Usually that does not require another massive translation session, unless the new version is significantly altered or expanded. The big capital demand to start up Rosetta Stone and Pimsleur produce tools with lasting value. Robert Fairbanks succeeded in getting Elementary Ojibwe developed for Pimsleur—and now we need to expand the scope and depth of that work by developing Intermediate and Advanced Ojibwe.

Just this year, the Mille Lacs Band of Ojibwe committed to producing six years of Rosetta Stone learning modules for Ojibwe. The financial investment for this undertaking is historic—Ojibwe will be the first indigenous language to develop this many years of material. The band wrote Rosetta a huge check with no regrets because Mille Lacs band members can see the value of having their living speakers be able to teach people for hundreds of years to come through the tools they will develop with Rosetta. Mille Lacs will retain all copyrights and all profits from sales of what will be produced and can even repurpose audio and video material used to develop Rosetta for other Ojibwe publications. When the material is published, six years of sequenced language classes will push to every band member's phone through the technological interface.

You will need to decide what to publish, what not to publish, and how to get it published. Every tribe is different, yet even within any given language universe there will be differences of opinion and perspective. The publication of sacred knowledge is tricky and often frowned upon by many tribal people, so proceed with caution and proceed with your elders guiding you all along the way. Some tribes, like the Lakota, tend to be more open, and speakers will rarely object to anything being published in the tribal language. Others, like the Pueblo communities of New Mexico, often object to *anything* being published in Tiwa, Tewa, or Towa. They even object to teaching the language in schools in some places. You cannot do this work without your community. Don't worry about pleasing everybody, but do take the pulse of your people and gather some support—create consensus if you can—about how to proceed. I have been careful not to publish Ojibwe ceremonial texts. As someone who officiates at many ceremonies, I have come to realize that for our ceremonies to function best, we need to send our people to their spiritual leaders, not go around them by consulting a book. It is important for people to go through ceremonies, not to give them a shortcut to content outside of the appropriate context. For us, tobacco, food, and other gifts accompany a request for sacred knowledge. Books aren't the place to get that. And the anthropologists just don't do us any favors here. Most of our ceremonies are about not only doing what is right by the spirits but also doing what is right by the people we want to go to ceremonies. For many reasons, I do not want to publish something that would be truly offensive or off-putting to our people.

I believe in the power of TL-immersion and monolingual TL publications, but as your effort matures, there is a value to expanding into other areas of language development. While the Ojibwe-medium schools need monolingual Ojibwe material, there is a value to bilingual material too. While English can be a crutch because people read it—and they often read it more than the tribal-language material—it can also reach people who otherwise wouldn't even start to lean in and support your efforts. You need both, so don't neglect any needs as you build a body of materials. Some of the important stuff for tribal-language-medium schools includes dictionaries that are not English-to-tribal-language, but tribal-language word lists with tribal-language definitions; and also literature of every possible kind. We need movies and television shows for kids and adults. Some tribal-language groups have obtained permission to develop voice-overs on Disney movies, and that's a great start, but we want to move in the direction of creating our own materials. Aboriginal Peoples Television Network in Canada has done a lot of tribal-language programming in Cree and Ojibwe, including *Tipi Tales* and *Sharing Circle*.

When it comes to getting published, there are advantages and disadvantages to almost every option out there. A lot of people self-publish. It's easier than it has ever been. You can write up your material, put it in a PDF, and publish it within a few minutes, with an ISBN and Amazon listing. We have used Lulu, although there are many other firms that can help you do this. Then all you have to do is share the link, and people can order copies of your publication on Amazon, which show up at their doorsteps within a week or so. It costs very little to get set up. You can set the price for your book and collect the

|||||||||||||||||||||||||||||||||||||||||||||||||||||||||||||||||||||||||||||||||||||||||||||||||||||||||||||||||||||||||||||||||||||||||||

money—minus a healthy cut for Amazon—via check or direct deposit to your checking account. You can also order copies for yourself, to keep, share, or sell at cost. Nice. There are disadvantages to this method, however, and they should not be taken lightly. The problem people have today is not finding information but finding which information they should pay attention to. Your work can be lost in a deluge of unreliable stuff. You get no marketing support, and you will sell primarily to your family and closest friends—it's very easy to be ignored beyond your immediate circle. Yet this venue can get you started if you can't find an established press to work with, and it can provide a reliable way to archive and keep accessible your work. It's also fast.

You can also work to develop your own press, or with others who are interested in developing a press. It's a huge job. Most small businesses fail, so success is hardly guaranteed. But the effort can be very empowering. Sometimes start-up presses can be really accommodating to our elders and the quality of their products can be great. But sometimes they have limited marketing (a listing on Amazon is crucial for getting a book to those who don't know you), or they are slow to handle orders for classroom use. Make informed decisions and you will do fine.

I have also published with larger presses like the Minnesota Historical Society and National Geographic. A lot of tribal language groups have struggled to get traction in these places. Every press needs to know that what they publish will sell, and if your language is small, it sometimes takes extra work; scholarly presses, which specialize in short-run books for specialized audiences, may be your best bet. We used to have to work hard to prove that Ojibwe language material had a market. But the *Concise Dictionary of Minnesota Ojibwe* has sold around forty thousand copies and *Living Our Language: Ojibwe Tales and Oral Histories* has sold around five thousand copies. Since most academic press publications sell fewer than a thousand copies, those are good numbers.

Once there is an established market for a book, it is easier to get a publisher's attention. There are huge advantages to working with a professional publisher. They edit your stuff—that makes it better. They design, market, and promote your stuff—that makes it sell better. They distribute your stuff to bookstores (at least, to those who will carry books in tribal languages) and reliably ship orders to teachers and schools—that improves sales and access. And they keep your stuff in print for sustained access over time. Your work will be more trusted by academics and people who give out book awards. All that adds to the ethos of your endeavor. You do lose some control over the production process, and you get a royalty that is only a small percentage of the net profit made on your hard work. You also have to help your elders navigate a bureaucracy they will naturally distrust, and you have to be persistent and patient with the process. But in the end, professional publication of your work advances most effectively the language you love.

*   *   *

There are organizations that can really help you get a jump start on resource development. The Indigenous Language Institute in particular will bring a team to your community and pair up with your team members so you can develop books and movie shorts with one-on-one guidance. They know the technology and process well. You know your language. I've seen them help generate genuine momentum when people were floundering around trying to get material out there. They are a nonprofit but they pay their staff, so most of what they do is fee-for-service work. It's worth writing their services into your next grant.

Some non-Native organizations can assist, as well. The Center for Advanced Research on Language Acquisition (CARLA) offers trainings in immersion-teaching pedagogy, statistical resources, research on the impact of language learning on cognitive function, and tools for assessing language development for less commonly taught languages. They have a dedicated staff. If they can't answer your questions or do your training, they can often help connect you to someone who can. Waadookodaading and other Ojibwe-medium schools use their services to train their staff. Other university programs—some populated with Native folks and some not—also often offer trainings and certifications that can have real value in building your team's knowledge as well as its credentials.

In addition to big national organizations like ILI and CARLA, there are regional groups that can often have a big impact on your efforts. Usually the First Nations within a given treaty area or the tribes in a particular state have a mechanism for shared conversation, advocacy, and sometimes cooperative effort around language and culture. The work of the Truth and Reconciliation Commission (TRC) in Canada will result in a significant allocation of funds, some of which will be administered regionally. The TRC could not address all the damage done to Canada's indigenous people, but it is a start in a long-overdue and much-needed effort to address historical injustice there, including language loss. In Wisconsin and Minnesota, Ojibwe, Dakota, Ho-Chunk, Oneida, Potawatomi, Menominee, and other tribes have worked together to advocate for language revitalization. The Dakota-Ojibwe Alliance helped advocate for the Bdote Learning Center, a tribal-language-medium public charter school in the Twin Cities that has an immersion wing for both Dakota and Ojibwe.

The Hawaiians, whom I mention often and look to frequently for guidance on how language revitalization is done, are very willing to share their strategic knowledge with other serious revitalization efforts. They currently mentor and train Ojibwe folks with a combination of trainings in Hilo and sustained communication through email and on the web. Their mentorship as well as trainings have been instrumental in accelerating our efforts in many places. The Maori, who have a unique political dynamic that empowers their language and culture revitalization, also have a lot of acumen and the will to help. And tribes in the United States and Canada that have found success are often willing to share their knowledge with, and mentor, other groups. The Cherokee, Mohawk, and Blackfeet have been especially generous. The Akwesasne Freedom School, for Mohawk, and the Piegan Institute, for Blackfeet, are well established and successful. If you want to have success, studying what doesn't work can only take you so far. Studying what does work can take you further, even though no two groups will have exactly the same strengths and challenges. Pay attention to the truly successful pioneers in indigenous-language revitalization. They have a lot to teach.

I have done a lot of work over the years for Waadookodaading Ojibwe Language Institute in Reserve, Wisconsin. Their entire staff is frequently assessed on Ojibwe language fluency, literacy, and use of immersion-based pedagogical approaches. The kids are regularly evaluated for Ojibwe fluency, literacy, and core academic standards. I usually did classroom visits and staff evaluations. It gave me a new view on what really works there.

At one of my early visits, I was stunned by the success of the program for four-year-olds. The staff had cobbled together funding for an early-childhood initiative, and really thought through what would give them the most bang for their buck. The second-grade science standards said that children needed to know the life cycle of an insect. So instead of just putting speakers in front of the four-year-olds and working on socialization, they carefully planned the entire classroom. Puzzles and basic games showed the metamorphosis of a butterfly, reinforcing core academic content being scaffolded up in the later grades. I watched with great fascination what transpired during circle time. A four-year-old child ran the circle. He asked the other children, "Aaniin ezhiwebak agwajiing noongom? (What's going on with the weather today?)" Someone raised a hand and said, "Ani-zaagaate." The kid running the circle turned to a felt board behind him and put up an image of the sun peeking out from behind the clouds. "Mii gwayak. Awegodogwen geyaabi? Noodin ina? (That's right. What else? Is it windy?)" "Enh. Mashkawaanimad. (Yes. There's a strong wind.)" Circle time lasted about half an hour. The kids did all the talking. There was no English. And those kids were operating in a language their parents do not know or routinely use at home. They were *age four*. It was inspiring to see how much they knew after six months in an Ojibwe-medium learning environment.

Waadookodaading uses an integrated curriculum, meaning that the science, health, mathematics, and social studies material is woven together. For example, they take the entire school to harvest wild rice. Everything is run in Ojibwe. Everyone would offer tobacco for the harvest in accordance with Ojibwe cultural practice. If someone might ask how much rice can fit in a canoe, the older kids would measure and calculate the size of one rectangle in the center of the canoe and two triangles at the ends, do the math, and then fill the canoe with water to check measurements. The younger kids would study the life cycle of a rice plant. The older kids would measure water-tension levels. They all harvest the rice, bring it to the school, parch it, and winnow it. Then they have a feast. Everyone brings some rice home to their families and learns the power of sharing, cooperative effort, and providing for loved ones. Back at school the teacher asks about the nutritional content for a serving of wild rice, what it means to call this a superfood, and what a staple food source is. Then comes the math. If this is a staple food, how much would one person eat in a year in a historic Ojibwe community? If there were 540 people in one village and 720 in the next, how much rice would each community need for a year? Then they would graph harvest levels. If the yield in some years was higher than others, how much rice would need to be harvested and retained each year to guarantee the same level of provisions over time to sustain this population? Then the kids would look at each other in amazement. "Wow, our ancestors did that?" Instead of internalizing shame and marginalization through their education, they were inspired, and proud of who they are and have been for all these generations.

* * *

Navigating the quagmire of rules, regulations, agencies, and programs required for launching and sustaining a successful language-revitalization effort is no small undertaking. Federal, state, provincial, and municipal governments all have something to say about nonprofits, grants, zoning for any buildings you want to use, and a host of other issues. The federal governments in the United States and Canada, and state governments in the United States, have requirements for what must be taught, when, and sometimes how. Filing taxes is a huge job, and accounting firms are expensive. You can't afford to mess it up, but it is sometimes hard to afford the help you really need.

Darrell Kipp's advice is really sound. His pamphlet, "Encouragement, Guidance, Insights, and Lessons Learned for Native Language Activists Developing Their Own Tribal Language Programs," is an invaluable resource. He said that at the Piegan Institute, which he founded to advance the Blackfoot language, they ask for an audit on their taxes every year. Even if the government has no interest in auditing them, they request one. The extra time and attention to detail do two things for them. First, they develop accountability habits that create records beyond reproach; they are ethical, detailed, properly compiled, and thorough. And second, they build so much trust with tax authorities and granting authorities that the institute's reputation is unassailable. Now the government usually refuses to audit them. And with the push of a button they can produce whatever kind of report is needed for whatever kind of grant they want to land.

You need to maintain the highest standards of excellence. Within our communities—and especially outside of our communities—there are many people who will have no faith in what you do. Some are just looking for an excuse to punch holes in the canoes we are using to carry our kids to fluency. Don't give them spears or they'll use them on your canoe. Keep the best records. Be perfectly ethical, appropriate, and timely. Go way beyond expectations and nobody will ever be disappointed. The work you do to maintain this excellence will take some of your precious time, but the extra lifting will make you extra strong.

When it comes to rules and standards, meet and surpass the marks set by the government and other authorities that have relevance to your work. Develop and show the data. The data is not to make our elders happy; it is to keep the money flowing and the doors open so you can teach the language to our kids. *That* will make our elders happy. Learn the tools of the trade, and make them work for you. Don't be a slave to someone else's tools.

You can fight against state educational standards every day, and you will lose. Those standards are full of problems and inconsistencies that drive everyone nuts. For the most part, politicians make terrible educators, and politicians exert a lot of influence on those standards. But if you take per-pupil funding from a government, which is the meat and potatoes of most funding for public, private, and charter schools in the United States, you will be held accountable to those standards. Even if you homeschool, you have to answer to some standards. Fight for changes in the standards, yes. But your energy is precious and your time is limited; it will be best spent if you use it figuring out how to make those standards work for you. Within the guidelines, there is plenty of room to do exactly what you need to do—speak the language you love to your kids all day, every day, while teaching them the content required by the standards. That way they will get the education everyone expects you to give them and the language you want them to know.

* * *

As you deliver on the standards, don't forget who you are or how to be. Educate your way. Indigenize the tools you use. Teach within your value frameworks. Use your teaching and cultural practices. Develop indigenous assessments. Develop indigenous spaces. And, if you can, avoid using colonized spaces.

I know there is a rich history at places like Haskell, now Haskell Indian Nations University, in Lawrence, Kansas. But that old residential boarding school, with graveyards for the kids, is a place with complicated memories and mixed spiritual energy. I understand wanting to convert it to a tribal space and taking pride in that, but I'd recommend not using old churches and boarding schools for that purpose. Develop fresh spaces with nothing but good history, filled with laughter and devoted to healing our kids and people. In many tribal communities, there is a diversity of faith traditions. Even in places like Oklahoma, where much of the tribal population is Baptist or Methodist, there are many people who follow, or are trying to revitalize, traditional, indigenous religious beliefs and practices and others who participate in the Native American Church. For some of them, an old, Christian religious building can be off-putting or even offensive. If you bring conflict-inspiring choices into the center of your language space, you will have conflict in the center of your language space. The work is hard enough without that.

When you do build places and spaces for your work, build the best you can. Use the highest standards available—federal, state, tribal, and programmatic. Have a high square-footage-to-expected-student ratio. Love our earth mother. Spend on the extra technology to build to environmental standards that will make our people proud. Be an example to the rest of the world, and tread lightly on our planet. Honor our values in everything you do. Have the best specifications to manage the environmental challenges in your area—floods, tornadoes, fire, and so forth. Keep our kids safe. Be state of the art.

I toured the Cherokee-medium school at Tahlequah and was really impressed with classroom layouts. One of the kindergarten rooms had a bunk bed in one corner, a library nook in another, a circle-time floor mat, tables and chair to one side, a white board on the other, class pets by the window, and a small greenhouse. One teacher and one paraprofessional could run eight learning stations simultaneously, each with different activities and different levels of challenge, without losing their minds. When there is a need to be attentive to differentiated instruction, which includes many children with IEPs (Individualized Education Plans) and perhaps transfer students with different levels of ability, classroom layout can help or hurt your efforts. The details matter.

Inside these buildings, work hard to develop the funding needed to make what happens there the best it can be. Keep a high teacher-to-student ratio. Pay your teachers well so you can attract and retain the best. For most tribal-language groups, just finding Native teachers is hard. Finding Native teachers who have full credentials and are fluent in your tribal language is even harder. Pay them right or they will leave. We operate with our values, but we operate in a non-Native world too. Money is a tool to provide for those we love. If someone else can pay your people more than you, you risk losing them. Sometimes you spend years investing in a team member's development and credentials and then see them jump ship. Keep them incentivized to stay, but if someone does jump out, wish them well. Keep reaching out. Honor them and invite them back. Preserving those relationships helps improve the chances that they will continue to contribute and come back to you. Mind the money. Mind the relationships. Both things matter.

Encourage and financially support the development of your team members. Do lots of professional development. If they don't have all the credentials and certifications, support their efforts to take weekend or summer college classes to fill in the gaps, and help them be able to travel to do so. Allow for sabbaticals, if they make sense, to beef up their résumés. All these things improve their performance in front of the kids and help you demonstrate to the rest of the world that you are rigorous and real.

A lot of tribal-language-medium schools work best when there are fluent first speakers of your language in front of your kids. Those speakers usually don't have credentials. Expecting an eighty-year-old speaker to go back to college, finish a degree, and come work for you for several more years isn't realistic. Put that speaker in front of the kids anyway. Use elder speakers as much as possible. Treat them as equals, not subordinates. Don't make them teacher aides or paraprofessionals. Pay them teacher wages. Honor their knowledge, respect their limitations, and put them at the center of the work. Some states allow for eminence credentials. Minnesota has a protocol for this that we have used with Ojibwe teachers. If someone can demonstrate eminent knowledge of our language and culture, there is a process to get it recognized by the Department of Education, which allows them to teach. Help your folks get those credentials.

Developing credentials for the team you are assembling is a short-term effort to get started and build your team. In the long term, we need to develop our own teacher-training and accreditation programs. This is where colleges and universities can provide the biggest impact. Using Jim Collins's metaphor from *Good to Great*, we can move from a doom loop to a flywheel when we figure out how to have a complete pipeline for language growth, beginning with day care and followed by elementary school, middle school, high school, and college. A doom loop is a cycle of despair, poverty, or ineffectiveness. A flywheel is a weighted windmill that gains momentum and sustains it with relative ease. This is critical to the successful language-revitalization work in Hawaii. A student can be taught entirely in Hawaiian, from early childhood through college, obtain their teaching degree in Hawaiian, and come back to teach in the Hawaiian-medium schools. It's a big job to build

collegiate teacher-training programs, especially ones delivered entirely in your language. But that should be the goal. It
can uncork growth in multiple key areas: successfully scaling
up the development of second-language learners into fluent
speakers; getting sufficient numbers of qualified, credentialed,
fluent teachers; and developing partnerships between all levels
of the educational pipeline.

I have long dreamed of developing this at Bemidji State University, where I teach. I want to have an early-childhood immersion program, all Ojibwe-medium, on campus. It would serve
multiple purposes: day care for the children of our university
students, a model of early-childhood Ojibwe-medium education, an employment opportunity for our university students
in the Ojibwe program, and a hands-on training ground for our
students in how to do immersion pedagogy. We would then
build an entire Ojibwe-language teacher-training program for
Ojibwe-medium education. It would recruit and credential college students and send them into the world to populate the
growing Ojibwe-medium efforts underway in Wisconsin, Minnesota, and Ontario, with the potential to expand those efforts
into Ojibwe spaces in North Dakota and Manitoba as well. For
our efforts in Ojibwe country, this is a critical need. A shortage
of Ojibwe teachers is the biggest single obstacle to expansion
of the Ojibwe-medium K-12 effort.

* * *

And then there are the parents. I watched with both horror and fascination the efficacy of the parental volunteer
effort to support my daughter's hockey program. The lessons
I have learned there have surprising application to language
revitalization. Bemidji is a big hockey town. But most of the
families in our area have limited financial means. Hockey is

expensive—equipment, travel, and the program itself. The program expected a lot of the parents. To participate in hockey, we had to write a big check. If we didn't volunteer a certain number of hours, they cashed the check. A dad complained at one of the parent meetings that he was a single parent and had a demanding job that made it impossible for him to volunteer the hours being asked of him. The response of the program folks seemed almost insensitive to me at first: "Well, you have a kid in hockey. Find a surrogate. Get grandma to help. Hire a teenager to work concessions in your place. You still have to cover your hours one way or another." He did. And I could see later how if one guy got out of volunteering his hours, a lot of people would do the same.

It's the same for a serious language revitalization effort: it only works if the parents are fully invested in what you are doing. All too often, parents want to warehouse their kids at school. You need to expect more from them. Require volunteer time, and financially incentivize it. The Piegan Institute requires tuition payment. They work hard to help financially strapped families, but everyone there has to pitch in. Waadookodaading requires all parents to take Ojibwe classes once each week so they can reinforce at home what's happening with the kids in school. Participation in your efforts should be viewed as a privilege that comes with a serious commitment from everyone—students, parents, teachers, staff, and community.

We have some families that experience legitimate and serious frustration with the academic choices their children face in public, private, and charter schools. We all have those frustrations. They extend beyond academics to social experiences, discipline, policies and procedures, school environment, and the climate of racial intolerance experienced in many places.

Sometimes families will want their kids to go to your school to get a respite from all of that, without being really committed to language and culture. Take the time to set the record straight when you onboard new kids. Many language programs have matriculation processes and ceremonies in which the families and school staff exchange promises to love and nurture the student and support one another's efforts to raise the child in a target-language learning environment at school and at home. These experiences can be really powerful and have a huge impact on reciprocal respect and ownership of language learning. Your program is not a dropout program. It's not a remedial program. It's not dumbed down. Expect great effort and sustained engagement from your students, parents, and staff, and you will get the most out of everyone.

* * *

Kids usually spend much of the first couple years in school learning social skills and routines. When they learn it all in English, their English improves. By seventh grade, students are learning formally about the language they already speak and seeing it in a new way. You will need to do this with your language as well. With target-language-medium education, the key is using the language you want the students to know to teach them everything.

Hundreds of years of educational evolution in both indigenous and nonindigenous spaces has produced huge bodies of knowledge and lots of deep thinking about how people learn, the most effective ways to sequence certain kinds of learning, and how to scaffold skill-building (learn this, then this, and you can do that). Take the best we have to offer in indigenous space and the best that is coming out of mainstream education and get rigorous about learning. We are—rightly—so used to fighting the systems of oppression that we often fail to see what kinds of thinking and teaching actually can best serve our purposes. For example, many language programs fail because at kindergarten someone is teaching a list of animals and how to count to ten and after a dozen years of language enrichment, by grade twelve, they are still teaching the same thing.

A solid language-learning effort will have a scope: it will identify a broad array of skills and types of language use and knowledge and hit on all of them each year throughout a kid's education. The guidelines for language learning published by the American Council on the Teaching of Foreign Languages (ACTFL) can be very helpful. They identify different kinds of language knowledge: interpersonal (conversation), interpretive (listening and reading), and presentational (speaking and writing). Within each of these categories, ACTFL identifies other types of knowledge: use of commands, literary analysis, storytelling, and more. If someone only knows how to tell someone else to come to eat or go to the bathroom, they will be lost when another person tells a story. Attending to the full scope of language skills can significantly improve the delivery of the goods to students and outcomes for real fluency.

Identify objectives and targets. What do you want students to know by third grade? Be specific across the entire scope of language skills you want them to have. Look at expectations for other established language-learning efforts and adapt their successful strategies for your learning environment. Set benchmarks for those objectives and assess your students along the way so you can track progress and see what's working well and what isn't. Then adjust what you are doing. This keeps every part of the effort accountable and improves your chances of meeting stated objectives and showing the outcomes that will justify your existence and keep you growing.

* * *

Eventually, you will have to make it rain money to sustain and grow your efforts. I think the money is too highly prioritized in the hierarchy of needs in a lot of places. After all, a well-funded but poorly developed language program is still going to underperform. There is an adage often quoted by personal finance gurus like Suze Orman: "Money is like health. Having it is no guarantee of happiness, but the absence of it can make you miserable."[8] Once you have identified your language needs and goals and started developing a team, you do have to make the money flow to build the infrastructure for language revitalization.

There is a science and an art to raising money, and there are different types of funding available: private donations, government grants, nonprofit grants, tribal funds, and per-pupil funds from state governments, bonding bills, and tuition. Different funds can be directed—and are sometimes restricted—to operating support, endowments, scholarships, and infrastructure. It's not simple.

Don't chase grants just to find money; you'll end up writing grants that will create work outside of your main mission just because it's easier to get money for someone else's priorities. First, identify all your needs and wants and sculpt a plan to meet them. You can be opportunistic within the framework of your dreams; you just don't want to get pulled away from your dreams because of the money.

One of the great secrets about successful fund-raising, whether it is in the form of grants or endowments, is that most people do not give money to people, programs, and places that need the money most. Millions of people are starving to death while you read this. They could use some money, some food, some trucks to get the food to where they live, but they get ignored. Thousands of worthy causes don't and won't get funded. I am a graduate of Princeton University. It has all kinds of money and yet 96 percent of its alumni give money to the university. They don't give because Princeton needs the money; they give because they love the place and what it does. People fund strength, not need. They also give for various reasons. They may believe a university will responsibly steward their resources. They may believe in the mission of the place. They may want to look good. Perhaps they want to alleviate their feelings of guilt, because on a certain level they know their abundance wasn't acquired on a level playing field. Maybe they believe in karma, and doing some kind of good feels good. But getting them to believe in your kind of good is a different matter. People follow the herd. This is part of the science behind major capital campaigns and efforts to get grants. If a place or program has a great reputation, it will get more attention and more money.

Indigenous communities experience the particular pain of invisibility. We don't even make the data sets for education much of the time. That's why producing data and measuring your needs and progress is so important. One of the tricks to really getting money rolling in is combatting invisibility. Waadookodaading has had a lot of success with this because their academic data shows they've been more impactful on core academics than English-medium schools serving the same students. Two of their students sang at the Tribal Nations Conference in Washington, DC, in 2014, hosted by Barack Obama. The students met the Obamas, sang songs on hand drums at the event, and never spoke a word of English. It has not been easy, but over time, the school has leveraged their great reputation into real financial support, and that has helped them increase their capacity for growth. Develop a reputation. Do great work. Keep and share your data. Amplify your voice. Then leverage your voice and reputation by asking the right people and institutions for funding at the right time.

It is common to start fund-raising by applying for grants. Identify which programs and organizations give them, and learn what they are looking for. Develop great and unique proposals. Don't expect grant-givers to understand you or meet you where you are. Meet *them* where *they* are. Speak their language. If there is a foundation or nonprofit that specializes in interrupting cycles of systemic poverty, highlight in your application how your program will make that type of impact. If they specialize in high school retention and graduation, speak to how you will engage with that.

Be rigorous about grant writing. You can't miss deadlines or write sloppy proposals. Some of the tribes that are most effective at grant writing are not the ones with the greatest potential for language revitalization. They just know that *immersion* is a buzzword in the grant-making world. The Administration for Native Americans (ANA) is a big granting agency that has helped a lot of programs get started. But they seriously vet applications. You have to speak their language. You are competing with a lot of great programs and with programs not nearly as great as yours that are great at writing grants. Be wise. Be persistent. Listen to feedback from staff. Revise. Resubmit. Repeat.

Know who you are talking to and what they do. The Shakopee Mdewakanton Sioux Community routinely gets thousands of unsolicited requests for financial support. But most of the people sending those requests get no support, mainly because they do not bother to understand what Shakopee does. The requesters often waste everyone's time and treat grant writing like it's a lottery. Over 90 percent of Shakopee's giving is

‖‖‖

directly to tribes, and around 90 percent of it is for infrastructure, not for programmatic support. They are not much interested in funding anything else, so don't write them an unsolicited grant for program money. Instead, ask your tribe to bring
them an infrastructure request. Other tribal sources of funding
have different goals and different capacities.

Ask your tribe for money, but don't wait for their funding
to start your work. View that request as one of many that you
will make. If they don't come through, it should not break
you. Tribes usually have elections every two years, and leaders
have to respond to their constituents. They have many competing priorities—health, housing, and substance abuse. Stay
persistent, engaged, and supportive. Speak their language and
understand the dynamics at play in your community. Draw
connections between language revitalization and health, substance abuse prevention, and community cohesion. Tribes
won't come through for you all the time for every need, but
they will likely come through for you eventually. Remember:
Darrell Kipp finally received $200 from the Blackfeet tribe after
eight years of asking. That delay didn't stop the Blackfeet people from revitalizing their language or maintaining healthy
relationships with their tribal council, which has since then
been a major supporter of language revitalization.

A sustained language-revitalization effort will have sustained and reliable sources of financial support. Capital campaigns are sophisticated and time consuming, so this isn't the
place to start your effort. But endowments do have a place in a
mature effort, so prepare yourself to learn this game too. Most
capital campaigns have a pyramid—a few high-level, lead gifts,
a second tier of substantial, midlevel gifts, and then a broad
array of gifts from alumni, staff, friends, family, and the community. Leadership and relationships are critical to a successful

campaign. In the long run, the bigger your endowments, the less vulnerable you will be to the vicissitudes of tribal politics and grant cycles. You still go after those monies, but your base is stronger, more stable, and better poised to weather all potential challenges. And the stronger you grow, the more money you will attract, because—as we know—people give to perceived strength, not perceived need.

* * *

As you get started with your effort, you might be tempted to think that language revitalization is about language and culture, *period*. Politics might sound like a four-letter word, to be avoided at all costs. While I'd agree that you do not want toxic politics inside of your language community, you have to navigate the world that is right here, right now. Because that world is highly political, you will need to prepare a strategic political response. Thinking about a political strategy to support your language-revitalization effort requires great care. You cannot afford to get sidetracked from your core mission and work. Some people are better at this part of the work. Use the right messengers to deliver political messages. You don't want to just protest the oppression and challenges you face; you need to transform obstacles into opportunities.

The Ojibwe have a clan system, as do many other tribes. For us, each clan has a bird, fish, or animal that doubles as a marker for the families and as a spiritual guide for individuals. In former times, clan was a primary determinant of what kinds of positions people would be groomed for in society—spiritual leadership, medicinal knowledge, protection, chieftainship. Our chief clans were the loon and the crane. The loon, keeper of the beautiful voice, was the diplomat, and usually considered the lesser chief. The crane, keeper of the loud voice, represented command, and was usually considered the head chief. Interestingly, at treaty signings, the lesser chiefs spoke first and most voluminously. Often, they spoke for the first two weeks of negotiation. Once there was an understanding between the parties, then the cranes would speak, saying, "I think you understand us now. And here is how it's going to be." We tell people to lead with the loon but finish with the crane. Seek first to understand others and be understood. But in the end, be firm in your beliefs. If we lead with the crane, we chase everyone away from the table and then end up complaining about eating alone. Rather than seeking control, be diplomats first, then be ready to stand strong.

Our languages deserve primacy of place everywhere we go. You do not have to apologize for this. Follow your tribal language and cultural protocol. For us, we introduce ourselves in Ojibwe with our Native name, clan, and home community. We do this wherever we are in the world, and in the company of speakers of every language. The kids at Waadookodaading did this when they met the president of the United States. This is a cultural protocol, but it is also a political statement. If we are going to be indigenous first and foremost, then we should use our indigenous languages first and foremost. As we deepen revitalization, we should endeavor to use our tribal languages more than we use English—then we will be thinking in our indigenous mind-set the majority of the time.

We have to name and declare the primacy of our languages. Petition your tribe to declare your language the official language of your tribe. Prepare your explanations. Show them how many tribes have done this and give examples of their declarations. In Red Lake in 1918, Peter Graves initiated a formal declaration of Ojibwe (Chippewa) as the official language of the tribe:

The Chippewa language is the indigenous language of the Red Lake Band of Chippewa Indians. Since time immemorial, the Chippewa language has been, and will continue to be, *our mother or native tongue*, which is our natural instrument of thought and communication. The Chippewa language is the *national* language of the Red Lake Band of Chippewa in a political, social, and cultural sense. The Chippewa language is the *official* language of the Red Lake Band of Chippewa Indians of the Red Lake Reservation and may be used in the business of government—legislative, executive, and judicial. . . . We declare that the Chippewa language is a *living* and vital language that has the ability to match and even surpass any other in the world for expressiveness and beauty. Our language is capable of lexical expansion into modern conceptual fields of politics, economics, mathematics, and science. Be it known that the Chippewa language shall be recognized as our *first language*.[9]

Once you have convinced your tribal leadership to make an official language declaration, turn around and use that declaration to leverage their political and financial support. That can come in many forms. Ask them to change the names of all tribal programs into your indigenous language. Ask them to revamp all road signs and signage inside buildings. Push them to run more tribal operations in your language. Be intentional about all of it. This normalizes your language and provides multiple sources of sustained language support in the places frequented by your people.

Petition your tribe to mandate that all tribal employees take classes in the official language of the tribe—the Native employees and the white ones too. That action speaks to the importance of our languages but it also sends a message to employees that they are significant and valued and part of the team that will keep our languages and cultures alive. It's not about shaming anyone for something they don't know; it's about empowering them to know. Does that make white people uncomfortable? If so, that's okay. They work for your tribe. Does that make Native people uncomfortable? Sometimes. But when presented with loving and supportive language-learning opportunities, people will usually respond as you hope they will—by leaning into language learning.

Official language declarations do not belong only at the tribal level. It is vital that you be political about the language. Seek to get your language adopted formally by each tribe, but don't stop there—seek official declarations at municipal, state, provincial, and federal government levels as well. (Hawaiian, for example, is an official language for Hawaii along with English.) Then turn around and use the official status of the language to push for more funding. Request, make possible, and then demand that road signs, literature, and public announcements be made in these official languages. In New Zealand, the Maori have been especially successful with this. When the Hawaiians got started over thirty years ago, it was illegal to use their language in public schools. Language warriors got that law changed and then paid close attention to the political dimensions of their movement. They worked to have Hawaiian declared an official language for the entire state. Then they kept the pressure on. The state has just one school district, so as they pushed for more meaningful application of the declaration, they soon had Hawaiian language and culture threads woven into the state standards and curricular expectations. Many towns changed their names and renamed roads to reflect the accurate Hawaiian words. This helped normalize Hawaiian beyond *aloha* and *mahalo*, creating a more substantive set of norms and expectations for its use. It also made room for more social, political, and financial support of the Hawaiian-medium schools. In effect, they are working to re-indigenize the entire state.

Even very conservative states like Alaska and Montana have responded positively to careful political efforts in support of indigenous language and culture. Alaska has developed a full set of Native Alaskan culture and language standards from kindergarten through high school. Montana adopted into its state educational standards an "Indian-education-for-all" platform, which means that all students of all backgrounds in Montana have to learn about certain indigenous content. The state also supports teachers, with resources and guidance, to deliver on these expectations. These are impressive accomplishments. Politics is at play everywhere. You just have to get your finger on the pulse of your place and roll out your best, beautiful, diplomatic loon voice to get things started.

Because of the official findings of the Truth and Reconciliation Commission, Canadians broadly acknowledge the cultural genocide that Canada inflicted upon First Nations people. In response, most government functions and many private ones now begin with a formal land acknowledgment—a statement about the past and present indigenous ownership of the land. That creates visibility for indigenous issues, and opens the door for First Nations people to advocate for their language and culture objectives in a more receptive space.

National, state, provincial, and tribal efforts aren't the only theaters of political action on language. In Bemidji, where I live, we have had great success advocating for greater acceptance of the Ojibwe language throughout the community. Michael Meuers and Rachelle Houle, white allies who are concerned about racial justice and engineering a social, economic, and political environment hospitable to all, pushed for changes to signage throughout the city. They visited businesses and schools—warmly, openly, and invitingly. They did all the front work on advocacy. I stayed out of sight and fed them lists of words and translations. It was helpful to have white faces make the approach, because that reduced discomfort for white business owners who might otherwise have felt pressured, or feared being accused of racism if they declined—or just gave what might have come across as a bad answer. By making safe space around the requests, we got traction. Today, all the public and charter schools in the area display bilingual signage in Ojibwe and English. Most of the area businesses display welcome signs in Ojibwe. The university and the regional events center have bathroom and welcome signs in Ojibwe. Not to be outdone, the tribes closest to Bemidji—Red Lake, White Earth, and Leech Lake—have been busy changing road signs and names as well. We did even more comprehensive signage overhauls for the Sanford Hospital in Bemidji and the Harmony Food Cooperative.

A special point of pride in Bemidji was to see the Bemidji Police Department adopt bilingual signage as well, even writing "Ganawenjigeng miinawaa Naadamaageng (To Protect and Serve)" on all police cruisers in the city. These expansions of our language into shared space help normalize our language. Some people didn't even realize we had a living language. But in Bemidji, everyone knows we do.

The signage doesn't produce speakers, but it acculturates everyone to seeing the target language in public spaces. That means the language isn't used just for ceremonies. It sparks curiosity. For us, it says that you're in Ojibwe country now. That's good for everyone, not just the Ojibwe. And the white business owners and politicians are happy to build trust with Native constituents and customers.

At Bemidji State University, we developed custom, free, talking flash card programs and posters and embedded them on the university website. Michael Meuers keeps a kit of signage material for anyone interested. Other towns in the region, like Park Rapids and Grand Rapids, are adopting similar sign-age. White business owners thank me in Ojibwe for my busi-ness. This alone doesn't save a language, of course, but it is one more tool to advance that mission.

As you get going, there is work for everyone. No one per-son can do all the work. Pull people together for strategy ses-sions. Identify people interested in taking on leadership roles on different political fronts, in educational initiatives, and in fund-raising efforts. Identify people willing to take on differ-ent resource development tasks and see them through to com-pletion. Use a strengths-based approach. Do what you do best. And set up others to lead in areas where they are strongest. There is more than enough work for everybody.

*   *   *

It may make sense for you to create a conference to promote or showcase your efforts. Grad students and schoolteachers, who are used to filling out proposals and making presentations, will volunteer, but you need to find presenters who can really advance your agenda. You may have to seek out and persistently pursue the most accomplished folks in the field, who are rou-tinely inundated with presentation requests. The same goes for knowledgeable elders and culture carriers. They may be happy to participate, but they won't fill out an online application to do so. Some may expect you to pay them a personal visit and present tobacco or follow other cultural protocols just to get them to attend. Give them what they need to make your event or conference great. Seek out people who are doing what you want to do, but in different places. We have learned so much from the Maori, Hawaiian, Mohawk, Blackfeet, and Cherokee folks who were in this game before we got going with Ojibwe.

They have built the kind of roads you want to bring people to travel. Pay attention to what they say.

If you put together a larger event, you will have special people-management considerations. A lengthy award ceremony can mean half your folks leave early and wander the casino. Present a couple awards at each meal function, spread out across your entire event agenda, and you'll have better, sustained engagement with the ceremony. When you have more people, you have more English, so make sure you pick emcees and other event personnel who will help you maintain language discipline and effective use of time. There are lots of apps for electronic devices and web-based resources to help you make efficient use of everyone's time. Be professional. Run a tight ship. And keep your language and culture at the center of everything.

* * *

Finally, embrace your role as language warriors with humility, resilience, and awareness of your own limitations. Revitalizing a language is a huge undertaking. Remember that good ideas are not enough. You have to be careful with how you allocate your time. I've found this challenging. Everything I say yes to forces me to say no to something else. There is an opportunity cost every time I jump to answer my phone, email, or the steady stream of interruptions coming to my office. When I was starting my career, I answered yes to requests to review other people's books, giving lots of free feedback on their pet projects, and I sat on all kinds of committees and boards. This helped me learn a great deal about others—and make some good connections. But I had to learn the power of no. I had to learn how to delegate and to give up a lot of that earlier work to make time for the things only I can do. Doing this is not just about work. I have to make sure my schedule reflects my true values and priorities. I block out time for family dinners, kid events, and date nights and dance classes with my wife. If I let others run my ship, they'll have me all over the map and far from my central mission. Don't waste your time and don't let others waste your time. Set your own agenda. Own it.

You will have to summon different energies for this undertaking: building, teaching, gathering, and sharing. So much lifting can be exhausting. Because you will face adversity, you will also have to be a fighter, an activist, and an advocate. This can be taxing in a whole different way. Pay attention to your elders, as their support means everything. But their demands can be daunting and their personalities can be prickly. You'll have the kids too—hearts with legs, but full of nonstop energy and needs. Pace yourself. Mind your support base. And pick your battles carefully. You don't owe days of ruminating and responding to one hater on Facebook. Keep a thick skin. Think ahead. What will serve your mission best? Put your strength where it will have the greatest positive effect.

Remember that Indian country is small, and navigating it can be tricky business. That hater on Facebook today may be deciding on your grant tomorrow. Tend to your relationships. But don't tiptoe around on eggshells. The best way to destroy an enemy is to make him a friend.[10]

Remember that you are operating in a community, and communities are made of people. Perceptions matter and can generate or drive away support. Insist upon high ethical standards for your team. That includes their sexual behavior and the way they joke at the water cooler. Set a high standard for how they talk about race and sexual orientation. Put respect at the heart of what you do. You can't afford to offend or alienate anyone in your community. And you certainly can't afford staffing dramas or lawsuits. Within those confines, of course you should be who you are and tell the same to your team. Don't lose your sense of humor. Pray hard. Work hard. Laugh hard too.

Native people can be cliquish or clannish. But remember that you are trying to build a movement and schools and programs that will have staying power for a long time. You will have to survive multiple tribal election cycles. In local, state, and federal politics, you will have to work with Democrats and Republicans alike. You will need support from people who come from all kinds of faith traditions and language backgrounds. Make everything you build big enough for all the families in your community. Be here for the people seven generations from now—when nobody knows your names.

You are working in innovative space. Be adaptive. Do not pretend to have all the answers. You will go much further if you ask the right questions. That will engage others and bring out their strengths. It will show you who has the ability and willingness to help you. It provides for natural engagement.

Native people have been assaulted physically, sexually, emotionally, linguistically, and culturally for a long time. As you navigate the minefields of historical trauma and contemporary struggle, remember that your people are sensitive. Their fears and bad memories can be triggered by the smallest things. Half the tribal population lives off-reservation. Even on reservations, the fluency rate in most tribal languages is low. People worry about getting shamed. They worry about getting blamed. They don't want to get out-Indianed by anybody. They may downplay the importance of our languages if they don't know theirs, to protect themselves from this type of criticism. Be careful when you lay out the importance of your mission. Don't tell people that their lives have no meaning if they don't know their language. Instead, ask them what gives meaning to their lives. You will advance your mission and speak to people's hearts if you push them gently and with love to find deeper meaning in the words, ceremonies, and culture our people have fought for all these generations.

EYES FORWARD
AND YOUR FEET WILL FOLLOW

||||||||||||||||||||||||||||||||||||||||||||||||||||||||||||||||||||||||||||||||||||||||||||||||||||

LANGUAGE LEARNING IS A POWERFUL, DECOLONIZING, AND healing act. While we work to more deeply understand the previous chapters of our experiences, we also need to write the new chapters. And we need to have a view for the plotline seven generations ahead of us. Imagine a world where our people have their languages, cultures, health, and prosperity. Then build that reality. Keep your eyes forward and your feet will follow.

Darrell Kipp was fond of putting it plainly. He always encouraged language activists to *show* rather than *tell* the importance of language. With all the resistance we have endured over the years, it's easy to forget that the language has status. I often think of one of my great mentors, the late Anna Gibbs. For most of her life, she was ridiculed or ignored, undervalued in most every dimension of her being. She was often racially profiled. She peered out at the world through those big, Coke-bottle, Indian Health Service glasses, and one of her legs was shorter than the other. Her Ojibwe was great, but her English was a little clunky. She didn't do that well at school. She didn't have a lot of money. She was a woman in a world organized around male power and dominance. But by the end of her life, Anna

Gibbs was one of the most prominent members of her tribe. More than one thousand people attended her funeral, which featured a huge horse vanguard escorting her body to internment and representatives from many tribes. She went from unvalued to highly valued through her years of Ojibwe language and culture service and leadership.

Our tribal cultures are being reimagined all the time. There is tension about what defines us, about being ancient and modern, about embracing change and staying the same. As we forge ahead, we must remember who we are and who we are not. We must keep the language at the center of our lived world and identity. That valuing will be contagious in the best possible way.

It might seem unfair that we have to do so much lifting because so much of the damage to our languages and cultures has come from the outside. But here we are. Frederick Douglass said, "Power concedes nothing without a demand."[11] Paulo Freire says that no oppressor has ever liberated the oppressed. Change happens when people who have been oppressed demand their liberation and recruit oppressors as allies to change the condition of both. Language powerfully defines who we are and where we are going.

Language revitalization is nothing short of a pathway to liberation. When we shake off the yoke of colonization, we no longer have to be defined by that history. We don't become decolonized. We become liberated—unconquered. That should be our goal for every one of our children and all the children yet to be born over the next seven generations. I frequently reflect on the proverb Anna Gibbs quoted me when she talked about bringing our language and culture back: "Every time they tried to bury us, they didn't realize that we were the seeds."

I have so much to learn. I really feel like I'm just getting started on my personal journey to live my language and culture. There is more road ahead of me than there is behind. And for the Ojibwe people and our collective efforts to stabilize and revitalize our language and culture, we really are just emerging. We need to grow the Ojibwe-medium education efforts from middle school through high school and into teacher training. The future of our language depends on these efforts. There is so much to do and so much at stake.

At the same time that I am truly humbled by the momentous size of this undertaking, I am inspired by how far we have already come and our potential to go much further. I have days when I want to give up, and I have days when I know I never could. I lean on my friends and family on the tough days, and I lead on the good ones.

In August 2019 I was back in Round Lake for Medicine Dance. A huge windstorm had downed sixty trees on the ceremony grounds a week before the ceremony started. I had been sending emails and making phone calls to ask for help. Hundreds of people showed up, off and on, for the week before start-up. Fond du Lac sent a forestry crew. Bad River sent vans full of volunteers. We cleared the grounds and built a new wigwam for the ceremony. Soon the grounds were full of ceremony people, including many of the language warriors I have worked with for years, families whose children attend Waadookodaading, and many others. One of the preteen girls from Waadookodaading got tobacco to sing. As she took the drumstick and started to speak in flowing Ojibwe before singing her first song, a hush fell over the assembled lodge people, and when she was done—a chorus of war whoops. Her accomplishment was impressive intellectually and linguistically, but even more importantly, it sent a wave of positive energy through the crowd. Hearing our kids speak our language is powerful medicine, and it heals everyone.

This past spring I gathered my entire family to open our sugar bush, as we do every year. That seasonal harvest has been routine for me every year of my life, a constant that, even in the most tumultuous years, has woven a tapestry of life that keeps me feeling connected to the woods, my ancestors, and my living family. I have three grandchildren now, and it was so heartening to watch my daughter speaking Ojibwe to my grandchildren there. I had one of my sons tell the legend of the sugar bush. We passed tobacco, and my daughter spoke for about twenty minutes in Ojibwe, addressing the spirits and asking them to bless our endeavor. It was a good prayer. And as I thought back to my own upbringing and the unlikeliness that I would ever know anything about our language, I couldn't help but marvel at what had just happened. We built an intergenerational transmission of Ojibwe in a place and family that hadn't seen that since my great-grandmother was growing up. While any number of things might interrupt our opening the sugar bush like that—deaths, new jobs or relationships for my kids, land sales, or moving or changing values and use of time—I had to smile a teary smile. Persistence is power. I could never give up. And I don't think my children ever could either.

My family comes from a rough part of the rez. But we've had a lot of success—the kind that white folks identify as success. My youngest brother is a medical doctor. My sister is a lawyer and judge. My older brother and I both have PhDs, and we've published over twenty books between us. There are lots of grandchildren and even some great-grandchildren. Everyone is doing okay. Everyone asks my mom how she did that. In a world that brought so many people down all around us, how did she raise her kids to be like this?

Her answer always sticks with me. She says that she always believed in education, but by that she doesn't just mean education from books. She made sure that her children knew how to open a sugar bush, how to snare rabbits, where to go for ceremonies, how to use their Indian names in their language. And that made all the difference in the world, because nothing can stop an Indian who knows who he or she is.

As I think about where we all are and where we all could go, I tremble with anticipation. *Courage* is the will to face our history, to own the challenges before us, to pick up our cultural toolbox, and to take initiative. Who will preserve our cultural patrimony? Who will save our languages? Who will make sure that seven generations from now, our future generations will know who they are? The ones who will lead the way are the language warriors. They are the ones reading this book, building a future for their languages, praying, striving, and speaking their truth in their languages. They are you. I believe in this effort. And I believe in you.

NOTES
|||||||||||||||||||

1. George Carlin, *Life Is Worth Losing*, HBO comedy special, 2005.

2. Paul Wellstone, speech to the Sheet Metal Workers Union, 1999, as cited in Gary Cunningham, "We All Do Better When We All Do Better," *Minneapolis Star Tribune*, September 22, 2010.

3. Attributed to Albert Einstein, as cited in Matthew Kelly, *The Rhythm of Life: Living Every Day with Passion and Purpose* (New York: Fireside Books, 2004), 80.

4. Carl Jung, *Letters. Volume 1* (New York: Routledge and Kegan Paul, 1973), 33.

5. Margaret Mead, as cited in Donald Keys, *Earth at Omega: Passage to Planetization* (Boston: Branden Press, 1982), 79.

6. Darrell Kipp, "Encouragement, Guidance, Insights, and Lessons Learned for Native Language Activists Developing Their Own Tribal Language Programs," Piegan Institute, Browning, MT (St. Paul, MN: Grotto Foundation, 2000).

7. Attributed to Bill Lawrence, *Scrubs*.

8. Suze Orman, Daniel Kahneman, and even the Dalai Lama have used variations of this quote in their speeches and

published works, without an obvious original source to which it can be attributed.

9. "Language Policy for the Red Lake Band of Chippewa Indians," General Council of the Red Lake Band of Chippewa Indians, Red Lake Archives, 5–6; emphasis in the original.

10. This paraphrase of Abraham Lincoln's words was cited in Robert Greene, *The 48 Laws of Power* (New York: Penguin, 2000).

11. Frederick Douglass, "West India Emancipation," speech at Canandaigua, New York, August 3, 1857.

WORKS CITED
||||||||||||||||||||||||||||||||||||||||||||||

*All of Anton Treuer's books are listed
on his website: http://antontreuer.com.
Here are some of the others referenced in this book:*

Boyce, Duane. *The Anatomy of Peace: Resolving the Heart of Conflict.* San Francisco: Berrett-Koehler Publishers, 2006.

Brown, Brene. *Rising Strong: How the Ability to Reset Transforms the Way We Live, Love, Parent, and Lead.* New York: Random House, 2017.

Collins, Jim. *Good to Great: Why Some Companies Make the Leap . . . and Others Don't.* New York: Harper Collins, 2001.

Covey, Stephen R. *The Seven Habits of Highly Effective People.* 1989. Rev. ed: New York: Free Press, 2004.

DiAngelo, Robin. *White Fragility: Why It's So Hard for White People to Talk About Racism.* Boston: Beacon Press, 2018.

Freire, Paulo. *Pedagogy of the Oppressed.* 1970. Reprint: New York: Continuum, 2000.

Kegg, Maude. *Portage Lake: Memories of an Ojibwe Childhood.* Minneapolis: University of Minnesota Press, 1993.

Kipp, Darrell. "Encouragement, Guidance and Lessons Learned: 21 Years in the Trenches of Indigenous Language Revitalization." In *Indigenous Language Revitalization: Encouragement,*

Guidance and Lessons Learned, edited by Jon Reyhner and Louise Lockard, 1–9. Flagstaff: Northern Arizona University, 2017. Available: http://jan.ucc.nau.edu/~jar/ILR/ILR-1.pdf.

Nichols, John, and Earl Nyholm. *A Concise Dictionary of Minnesota Ojibwe*. Minneapolis: University of Minnesota Press, 1995.

Orman, Suze. *The Courage to Be Rich: Creating a Life of Material and Spiritual Abundance*. New York: Riverhead Books, 2002.

INDEX

IIIIIIIIIIIIIIIIIII

178

Index

|||||||||||||||||||||||||||||||||||||||||||||||||||||||||||||||||||||||||||||||||||||||||||||||||||||||||||||||||||||||||||||||||||||||||||||||||

||||||||||||||||||||||||||||||||||||||||||||||||||||||||||||||||||||||||||||||||||||||||||||||||||||||||||||||||||||||||||||||||||||||||||||||||||||

〰〰〰

||||||||||||||||||||||||||||||||||||||||||||||||||||||||||||||||||||||||||||||||||||||||||||||||||||||||||||||||||||||||||||||||||||||||||

||||||||||||||||||||||||||||||||||||||||||||||||||||||||||||||||||||||||||||||||||||||||||||||||||||||||||||||||||||||||||||||||||||||||||||||||||||||||||||||||||||||||||

183

Index

||||||||||||||||||||||||||||||||||||||||||||||||||||||||||||||||||||||||||||||||||||||||||||||||||||||||||||||||||||||||||||||||||||||||||||||||||||||||||||||

The Language Warrior's Manifesto was designed
and typeset by Judy Gilats in St. Paul, Minnesota.
The text face is Alda, designed by Berton Hasebe in 2008.